PICTURE FRAMING

by Vivian Carli Kistler C.P.F.

Library of Professional Picture Framing
Volume One
Picture Framing
By Vivian Carli Kistler C.P.F.

Published by Columba Publishing Co.
        Akron, Ohio

Copyright © 1987 by Vivian Carli Kistler
Revised Edition 1990
Printed in the United States of America
ISBN: 0-9-38655-11-6

Book Design by Ray Gedeon
Editors
        Vivian C. Kistler
        Sheri Leigh Galat
        Jennifer Vinson
Illustrators
        Margaret M. Meek
        Marla Strasburg
Photographer
        Robert Graetz

10   9   8   7   6   5

**THE LIBRARY OF PROFESSIONAL
PICTURE FRAMING**

CONTENTS

DEDICATED

to

Harvey Eisenstodt

William Humberg

Clyde Kistler

Jerry Maroney

for their guidance
and encouragement

PREFACE

The Library of Professional Picture Framing is designed to provide detailed information on the theory, materials and procedures of picture framing.

The first volume is a practical reference guide that deals with the basic elements of framing, from the history of period frames to the application of a dust-cover and screw eyes. The purpose of volume one is to give a solid background, providing an overview of framing as both a craft and an art form.

Other volumes in The Library will examine specific facets of picture framing in depth. These books will provide comprehensive coverage of the many techniques available to and practiced by the professional framer.

This is the book I needed in 1967 when I started my frame shop. I began like most other framers, with very little knowledge but plenty of guts. After all these years, I still don't know how to do everything — there are always new things to learn — but I do know how to track down any answers I need.

The methods presented here are all good practices, but hardly steadfast rules. Picture framing requires lots of creativity and practice. Working with different materials, on different equipment, under different conditions, each framer develops individual methods of framing.

Do you have methods you'd like to share with other framers? Please write me at P.O. Box 34110, Akron, Ohio 44333. Or see me at any ABC show or PPFA convention. We can only improve our profession by sharing our knowledge.

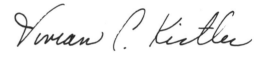

1
The History of Picture Frames

Framing has evolved from a basic desire to isolate artistic images, defining their space and establishing their boundaries, while also enhancing the images. The history of frames is a story of constant change and variety in an effort to accomplish these goals and satisfy popular fashion demands at the same time.

The frame as a painted decorative border is known from ancient Egypt, Greece, and Rome (on mosaics and wall paintings), and on the walls of European churches, where religious images are surrounded by bands of decoration similar to those found on ancient manuscript pages.

The first dimensional frames for paintings began around the 13th century, when paintings that were independent units — not painted directly on walls — became popular. These early "panel paintings" did not have frames in the modern sense. Instead, the picture was painted on a slightly hollowed-out wooden panel whose wooden rim became the frame. The rim was decorated to match the architectural style of the churches where these religious paintings were housed. Soon it became obvious that support was needed to protect the large painted panels from warping and splitting, so separate strips of wood were applied. These borders were still considered as part of the painting, and many decorations were added to them. These "Tabernacle frames" generally consisted of a thick base, long, vertical side columns (pilasters), and a broad cornice, sometimes accented with pointed spires. The section that housed the painting often featured a semicircular top. In framing, this flat-bottomed, rounded-top shape is called "Gothic" style. The great altar pieces of the 14th and 15th century churches were panel paintings, hinged together and braced with elaborately ornamented moulding.

With the acceptability of panel painting came the easel painting, which allowed the artist to work in a studio. Now frames were made separately from the painting, often created by the artists themselves, and usually finished before the final painting began. These frames were designed to be an extension of the painting. A style, symbol or shape from the artwork might be continued in the frame; names and dates appeared on portrait frames. This harmony between painting and frame was possible partly because of the varied skills of the artists, whose extensive education included everything from botany and architecture to gilding and color-mixing.

As the Renaissance moved forward, different types of frames evolved to display the wide variety of paintings commissioned not only by the Church, but also by wealthy merchants and nobles (who sought portraits as well as religious and mythological subjects). As with any art form, different areas of Europe developed their own styles of framing.

The Italians proved to be the early masters of the craft, and the beautiful frames of Italy influenced those of Spain, Germany, France, and the Netherlands. The basic Italian frame of the late 15th and early 16th centuries has been called the "border frame." It consisted of three sections — an inner lip of raised gold moulding; then a wide, flat band that was painted, embossed, or delicately engraved; and a raised outer moulding strip similar to the inner lip in decoration. These frames expressed restraint in design, the bright gilding sometimes softened with a thin overlay mixture of glue and pigment.

During the 16th century, the classical balance of the Renaissance frame began to fade and a trend towards complexity and excess emerged, characterized by rich carvings, and inlays of marble and precious stones. A decorative technique called "sgraffito" involved covering the gilded, flat band of the border frame with a layer of blue, red, or black tempera paint, then scratching out a pattern, such as leaves or vines, to reveal the gold underneath. A round form of frame called the "tondo" became popular — ornate carved wreaths of flowers or leaves, designed for circular paintings originally inspired by the Madonna and Child tomb medallions that were set into church walls.

Through the 16th century, Italian frames became thicker, the ornamentation larger and more dimensional. Elaborate scrollwork became common in framing (and in architecture as well). This style of frame was called "Sansovino" after Venetian architect Jacopo Sansovino. The border frame was still standard, but with so much decoration that the three sections were not clearly defined.

The Spanish version of the border frame resembled the Italian but was heavier-looking, with bolder carving and dark, deep-toned gold leafing. Another Spanish style used a broad, rounded moulding with large, carved patterns overall.

In Germany, the three-section frame was very highly decorated, not only on the two rims, but on the flat center as well — often embellished with coral, shells, and copper or ivory inlays.

In Holland, the variations were more distinctive. The typical Dutch border frame was of wide, dark wood, often painted black, and well suited to the austere Dutch interiors of the 16th century. But during the 17th century, peace and prosperity gave rise to a wealthy merchant class (shipping and banking merchants, especially) who patronized the arts. Now these dark frames featured imported tortoise-shell and ebony. Mechanically cut patterns of basketweave and rippled veneers were applied to flat surfaces of frames. Carved giltwood frames emerged to satisfy the showier interiors of the merchant class. The best known of these is the "Lutma" frame, named for goldsmith John Lutma. These frames were characterized by high-relief carvings in swirling designs, depicting flowers, birds, and various forms of shells and sea life.

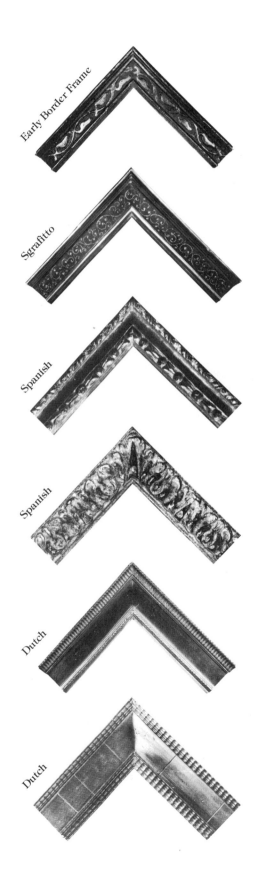

Early Border Frame

Sgrafitto

Spanish

Spanish

Dutch

Dutch

The rise of a monied middle class was also occurring in France, and French frames, many inspired by Italian styles, began to influence the framing world. These frames were designed more often by furniture makers than by artists, to coordinate with furniture styles. A greatly increased demand for frames led to semi-mass production, governed by the highly-organized craft guilds, resulting in an unprecedented consistency in style. Illustrated books about interiors were published and were popular — the designs they showed were widely copied and became another source of this new consistency.

The first identifiable frame of this period was the Louis XIII (1610-1643). A typical Louis XIII frame was characterized by shallow relief carving of leaves and flowers, generally in an overall design with unbroken lines. These frames were flattish and not very thick. Louis XIV frames (1643-1715) featured a distinctive innovation: clusters of ornamentation breaking the lines of decoration at the centers and corners of the frame.

Italian frames of this time often were updated variations of the border frame. One popular design was the "Maratta," in which the normally flat center panel was a gilded scoop, and the strips of moulding rose in sequence towards the outer edge of the frame.

By the end of the reign of Louis XIV, France rivaled and even dominated Italy as the center of European art, and the recently founded Academy of Painting and Sculpture (1663) became the recognized authority on framing. Frames were once again designed by artists, but continued to be produced by the Paris guilds.

The French Regency period (1715-1723) followed, and was an age of elegance and splendor. Regency frames displayed ornamentation made precise by beginning with general outlines in wood, which were then coated with layers of gesso and carved into fine detail. These finely detailed decorations, brightly gilded, were separated on the frame by spaces of plain moulding called "repos" (rests). These were the days of the gifted, Dutch-born Englishman Grinling Gibbons, who was one of the greatest woodcarvers in history. His rich, incredibly naturalistic carvings were highly valued, and he produced magnificent frames while he was Master Woodcarver to the Crown under both Charles II and George I of England.

This opulent period reached its height under Louis XV (1715-1774). Picture frames featured swirling, flowing designs, fitting the ideals of the Rococo style. A hallmark of this frame is the "pierced" or "perforated" design — graceful open loops of decoration adorning edges of the frame. The use of frames was wildly popular. They appeared on mirrors, screens, even sections of walls, and were copied in decorative borders on fabrics and book illustrations. This exuberant style was borrowed and modified in the frames of other areas. In England, for example, Thomas Chippendale integrated bamboo and other oriental themes into his fanciful designs, in response to the popularity of Chinese subjects at that time.

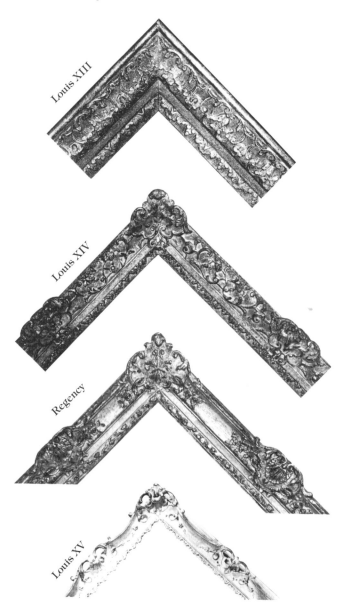

Louis XIII

Louis XIV

Regency

Louis XV

As is typical with all trends and fashions, there was eventually a reaction against this excessive style. In the mid-late 18th century a movement called Neoclassicism emerged, representing a revival of symmetry and simplicity. The discovery of the buried cities of Pompeii and Herculaneum provided authentic classical designs and motifs that were widely used in art of this period. This style, called Louis XVI (1774-1792), was expressed in picture frames with straight, continuous lines of precisely carved pearls, leaves, and ribbons, alternating with bands of plain moulding. These frames, along with the small oval frames which remained popular, were frequently crowned at the top by a carved bow with streaming ribbons, or a garland of flowers with trailing vines.

During the French Revolution, there were no notable advancements in French framing. Many old frames were destroyed, burned to salvage their gold leaf during the war. Following the Revolution, Napoleon's dictatorship brought about strong uniformity of style in interior design. The "Empire frame" was a gilded scoop style decorated with finely molded plaster-cast ornamentation, in a symmetrical design. Napoleon had almost every painting in the Louvre reframed in this rigid design, whether suited to the painting or not; many original frames were lost in the process.

As the 19th century continued, frame design became diluted and vague. Many were bad copies of Louis XIII or Louis XIV (called "barbizon frames"), usually brightly gilded. The plaster casting of ornamentation allowed for mass production, but tended to look harsh. Mouldings tended towards the wide and deep, with a preference for fanciness superseding all other considerations. There was little notable variation from country to country.

The frames of America were somewhat of an exception to this trend. Although the earliest frames in America followed European styles, or were actually brought from Europe, the rugged lifestyle experienced by many of the new settlers inspired more suitable frame designs. The earliest American contribution to framing was the plain, black, painted frame first seen around 1740, well-adapted to the simple, conservative colonial decor. Simple designs in natural wood finishes also appeared, thanks to the wide variety of wood types readily available. Eventually, small embellishments, such as a gilded inner lip, became popular.

By 1830 another original American style emerged — a plain, angular moulding with no embellishment or ornamentation, but a variety of tones of gilding, with some areas burnished and others unburnished.

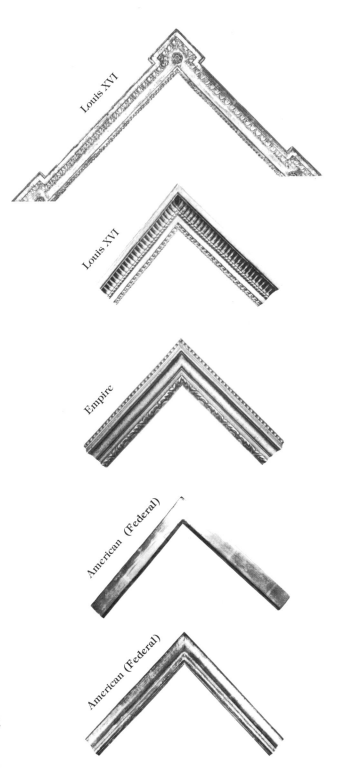

Louis XVI

Louis XVI

Empire

American (Federal)

American (Federal)

The great tide of immigration during the mid-late 19th century brought a period of great variety as new tools, talents, and artistic preferences were assimilated. Decorated frames became more popular. Economics and quantity demands led to a type called composition frame. Instead of carving ornamentation individually, the carver made a mold from which any number of pieces could be cast and adhered to a wooden frame.

Economics also encouraged a revival of silver gilding, especially a combination of silver leaf over gesso, coated with a red-orange lacquer producing a golden color much less costly than gold. There was also a revival of the heavily ornamented European style frames, mass-produced to accommodate ostentatious Victorian interiors.

The late 19th-early 20th century was a period of great freedom and variety in framing in America and Europe, as many artists reclaimed control of the harmony between painting and frame. As carved ornaments and jewels were once used for decoration, now burlap, cork, and printed paper decorated new frames.

After almost two centuries of nearly all frames being dark or gilded, the Impressionist artists of the late 1800s adopted a very new style. Since the orange tones of gold frames did not complement Impressionist colors, they chose instead a simple white frame, slightly tinted to soften starkness. George Seurat carried his pointillism style in painting to the white frame, covering it with dots of color similar to those in his painting. Degas also painted speckled borders to create a gentle transition from painting to frame. Other artists who experimented with this balance were James McNeill Whistler, who painted patterns on his frames (basketweave, fish scale, and other designs), and Thomas Eakins, who used mathematical symbols to decorate the frame for his portrait of Professor Henry Rowland.

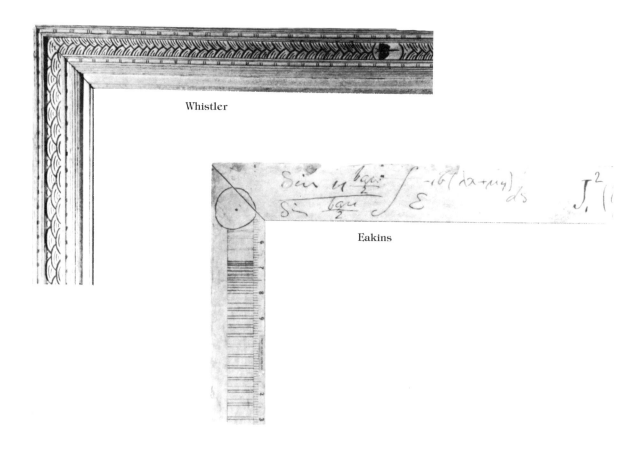

Whistler

Eakins

During the 20th century there has been renewed interest in the harmony between the picture, frame, and setting. New framing styles have evolved, using modern materials and satisfying contemporary tastes. The centerpiece of this style is the "minimal frame," a single, simple line of wood, plastic, or aluminum. The first aluminum frames (welded design) to reach public awareness were produced in the late 1950s for the Museum of Modern Art, and by 1968 the first pre-packaged kits of extruded aluminum sections were marketed nationally. The first plexiglass box frames, the ultimate in minimal framing, were also designed for the Museum of Modern Art.

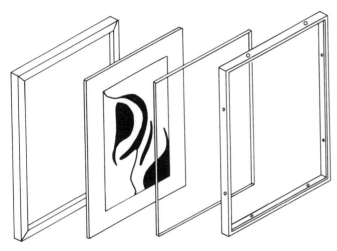

Early Welded Metal Frame with glass, matted art, and wooden strainer.

Throughout history, frames have reflected trends in art, architecture, and social fashion. To suit the incredibly diverse range of artwork and interior design that is concurrently popular today, we need, and do have available to us a tremendous variety of frame choices, representing everything from authentic reproductions of historical styles, to the laminated plastic, aluminum, and acrylic designs that are today's "period frames."

2

Moulding

Even though there are other options, such as metal and plastic, wood moulding still represents the largest percentage of sales. Mouldings are made from different types of woods, have different types of profiles, and are finished in various ways. These three variables make possible the tremendous selection of wood mouldings available to us as picture framers.

Manufacturing moulding can be a complicated process. At the minimum, preparing wood for frame moulding involves drying (naturally or with oven heat – kilns), shaping into desired profile, sanding, and finishing. Knowing about wood and how it is finished can make quite a difference when buying, cutting, and joining moulding, and when repairing frames.

Finishing refers to the various treatments performed on wood to give it the desired appearance. There are three basic types of finishes: Finishes that use and accentuate the natural grain of the wood; finishes that conceal the grain by covering it, as with paint; and finishes that give the wood a metallic look, as with gold leafing. These methods are often used in combination on a single moulding.

Mouldings are available in every style and quality, from those that only have one coat of spray paint, to those with fine furniture finishes that are hand-rubbed to a soft patina; from carefully burnished gilded styles to those with dozens of layers of glossy lacquer. With all these variables it's no wonder that framers have trouble getting four sticks of moulding to match! This is probably the most common complaint from a framer, and the most difficult problem for the manufacturer to deal with. You could find 25 manufacturers to provide you with a 3/4" half-round black moulding – but each would send you their own particular version. The variety of finishes would include everything from a single coat of paint on raw moulding, to paint applied several times and rubbed to a satin sheen, to paint sprayed over a gesso base.

Perhaps you have noticed a hard white (sometimes colored) coating under a painted moulding finish. This is called gesso. It is a ground applied to the wood to give it an ultra-smooth finish without all the sanding and sealing usually required on raw wood. The finished product is beautiful, but it does have drawbacks. It can chip, especially when cut with an electric saw, and these chips are very difficult to hide. If gesso-based moulding is dented, the finish cracks. Gesso is also very tough on chopper knives. Note – Gesso is not the same as "compo", which is a malleable compound used to make moulded ornamentation for period frames and traditional mouldings. Compo decoration can also chip during cutting.

Let's take a look at the raw material underneath all the fancy finishes. To really understand the properties of wood, we must begin with the growing of the tree. Wood is a hard, fibrous substance that grows beneath the bark of a tree or shrub. Wood is made of cellulose, lignin, hemicellulose, and extractives. The cellulose make up half of the wood by weight, and gives wood its strength and structure. Lignin binds the fibers of wood together. Hemicellulose is similar to both cellulose

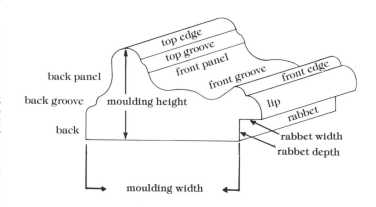

and lignin, but is less complex chemically. The extractives include fats, gums, oils, and coloring matter. The proportions of these substances varies among the different kinds of wood. The cellular structure also varies, which makes some woods heavy and some light, some stiff and some flexible, some plain and some colorful.

Wood is generally classified into two basic types, softwood and hardwood. These terms refer to types of trees, not literally the hardness of the wood. Softwood comes from conifer trees (cone-bearing), which usually have needle-like evergreen leaves. Hardwood comes from broad-leafed trees, most of which are deciduous — that is, they lose their leaves in autumn.

Temperatures, soils, and growing seasons differ. Rainfall varies, and wood swells and shrinks depending on how much moisture it loses or absorbs. The weight, consistency, grain, density, and color of wood are all affected by growing conditions.

Here is a brief overview of some of the wood types commonly used for picture frame moulding. For purposes of description in this listing, the terms "soft" and "hard" *do* refer to specific qualities of the wood, rather than to tree type.

BASSWOOD comes from the linden, a slow-growing tree common in the northern U.S. and Canada; the even color varies from cream to light brown; lightweight; soft; plain, even-textured grain that is easily worked and carved; finishes beautifully; the single best competitive advantage American manufacturers have over importers; the fine quality allows finishing directly on wood without gesso.

BANECK is imported from Brazil; it is similar to basswood, but has a more distinct grain; cream to light brown color; soft, with open pores; very stable, normally won't warp or twist, but must be specially kiln-dried to prevent infestation by powder-post beetles.

RAMIN is imported from Malaysia and Burma; consistent cream color, with walnut-like grain; very hard; high quality, with a grain that makes it ideal for most stains and finishes, including leafing and laquer; like basswood, good ramin requires no "filler coat" before finishing.

PINE is a very soft, inexpensive wood; strong grain, with no pores but distinct rings (knots); dents easily, but is basically strong; lightweight; stains easily and attractively; color usually varies from white to pale brown, but southern pine is very yellow, and hard.

OAK is heavy and very hard, making it difficult to cut; color ranges from almost white to light brown (white oak) and to reddish brown (red oak); pronounced grain that can be coarse, so tends to be used as a stained finish only, rather than as a base for other finishes.

The following are also used for frame moulding, though somewhat less frequently:

POPLAR is soft, lightweight, and close-grained; the color is whitish tinged with gray or green, often in streaks; plentiful, relatively fast-growing; inexpensive; some tendency to twist and warp; usually painted, rather than stained, because of the gray-green streaking; often used for liners, both raw and linen-covered;

accepts paint and other finishes well, so is sometimes used as a base for contemporary gold-leafing.

AMERICAN WALNUT is gray-brown to dark brown in color; very hard, difficult to work with; variety of graining, from straight to swirling; somewhat rare.

CHERRY is known for its attractive natural sheen, which can be rubbed to a high gloss; color is light to dark reddish-brown; very hard; distinct, straight, uniform grain.

MAHOGANY has a reddish color with light and dark irregularities that give it a beautiful, feathery grain when stained and polished; soft; lightweight; can be finished without staining.

BIRD'S EYE MAPLE is one of the few maples used for frame moulding; rare and expensive; very hard; medium brown with distinctive dark brown specks overall.

EXOTIC WOODS are a group of unusual woods, used occasionally for frame moulding because of their distinctive appearance; examples include red Brazilian rosewood and striped African zebrawood.

FINISHING PROCESS

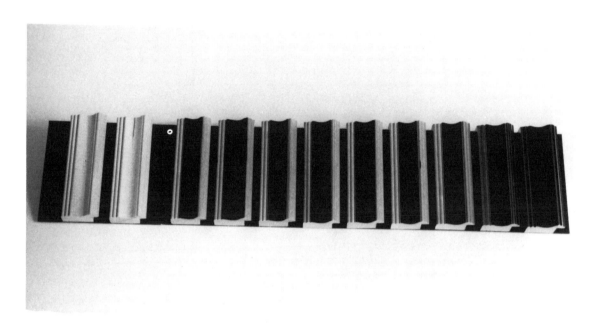

FINISHING MOULDING
OR
HOW COME THIS MOULDING COSTS SO MUCH?

The quality of moulding is determined by the type of wood used, how accurately it is milled, and how well it is finished.

The finest quality furniture finish is completed in eleven steps (shown above).

STEP 1 Basswood is milled to close specifications with knives that have been made to pattern this profile.

STEP 2 The exposed sides are sanded by machine while the remaining edges are sanded by hand.

STEP 3 The stain is applied by hand — not by spray or brush. Applying it by hand gives better control.

STEP 4 The first coat of lacquer is applied. You can feel a raised fuzz.

STEP 5 The fuzz is removed by sanding.

STEP 6 The second coat of lacquer is applied.

STEP 7 The third coat of lacquer is applied. You can see the "orange peel" build up.

STEP 8 The moulding is now hand rubbed to distribute the three coats of lacquer evenly.

STEP 9 a) The moulding is hand polished.
b) Seven more coats of lacquer are applied.
c) The area of the moulding that will receive the gold leaf will have 7 coats of shellac for the leaf base.

The moulding is then allowed to dry for a minimum of 48 hours.

STEP 10 a) Oil size is applied for the gold adhesion.
b) The leaf is applied by hand.
c) A sealing shellac is applied by hand.

STEP 11 The grooves are cleaned out and darkened with antiquing solution.

ORDERING MOULDING

Moulding comes in 5' to 16' sticks. Most often the length will depend on the type of wood it is made from — some trees grow taller than others. Moulding will arrive at your shop with a brown crepe ribbon wound around it, keeping it straight and making it easier to handle. More recently, some companies began using plastic wrapping, or brown kraft paper lined with a plastic coating. Wrappers provide protection against dirt and moisture. Excessive moisture changes the nature of wood, making clean cuts very difficult.

There are different ways to order moulding:

LENGTH means ordering footage to stock in your shop. Fifty feet of each moulding is a good amount to start with; you will get roughly six to eight frames from 50 feet of moulding. Of course, larger or smaller quantities may be purchased. Companies will offer price breaks depending on the amount of footage you buy. Buy only what you think you can use in the immediate future. Stocking moulding requires space and money — picture framers seldom have an excess of either.

When choosing mouldings to stock, get a well-rounded selection–something in each basic category, including stained wood patterns, gold and silver leaf, and black. Be careful about stocking trendy colors — they come and go quickly. Give yourself a range of widths and profiles, from ½" rounds to 2½" traditionals. The larger mouldings usually sell somewhat less frequently, so you may prefer to order them special from your supplier. This method of ordering is called Chop Service.

CHOP SERVICE is offered by some manufacturers and most distributors. This is how it works: A sample corner of the moulding hangs on the wall of your shop. A customer selects it for her frame job. You measure the frame job exactly and order the proper moulding from the supplier — "chopped." They will send you the four pieces of moulding needed for your frame, cut to the size you have requested. It is common practice for suppliers to add 1/16 of an inch to all measurements, to allow for expansion of the materials required in the fitting. For example, if you order a frame 16" x 20", the chop company will cut it 16-1/16" x 20-1/16". The chop should be delivered to you a few days after ordering.

Choosing mouldings from chop services expands the selection you can offer to customers. It also gives you an opportunity to "try out" a moulding before ordering it in length. There is a price difference between length and chop — chops do cost you more, but you save cutting time in your shop, and there is no waste in small, leftover scraps as there generally is with length moulding.

Some companies also offer **JOIN SERVICE.** You can order a moulding "chopped and joined," which means it will be assembled for you by the supplier.

This is a great idea if you do not have the proper equipment or skills to build frames yourself. It also comes in handy for large orders, difficult mouldings, or when your framer goes on vacation.

When it comes to choosing which companies to deal with, experience is always the best teacher. However, in the beginning look for a company that can offer you a good product, quick service, and perhaps a sales representative to call on you. Don't ignore the value of the sales representatives in this industry — they are very willing to help you and they are generally trustworthy. Since they will be calling on you often, they will give you their best — knowing they will have to face you again the next time they are back in town. They want to make you a repeat customer. They also attend the trade shows, and are good sources for the latest supplies and information.

You will notice that moulding manufacturers and suppliers usually offer a particular type of moulding, such as European imports, fancy period styles, or traditional domestic mouldings. Since companies tend to specialize, you will need to do business with two or three different companies to offer a well-rounded selection to your customers. But if you deal with too many companies, you will probably be placing small orders, making it difficult to meet the minimums required to place orders economically. Also, it is generally better to be an important customer to two or three companies, instead of being an occasional, one-frame customer to several companies.

You may want to stock ready-made frames in your shop. These come in every conceivable style and a wide range of sizes. They are made from many types of materials, including wood, pressed wood, expanded plastic, and metal. They are available empty, or complete with glass and backing. The most common standard sizes are:

5 x 7	11 x 14	20 x 24
8 x 10	12 x 16	22 x 28
8½ x 11	14 x 18	24 x 30
8 x 12	16 x 20	24 x 36
9 x 12	18 x 24	30 x 40

Some of the smaller sizes are available in oval frames. You may also want to stock a small selection of unusual ready-made frames such as round, octagon, or fan-shaped.

PROFILES OF WOOD MOULDINGS

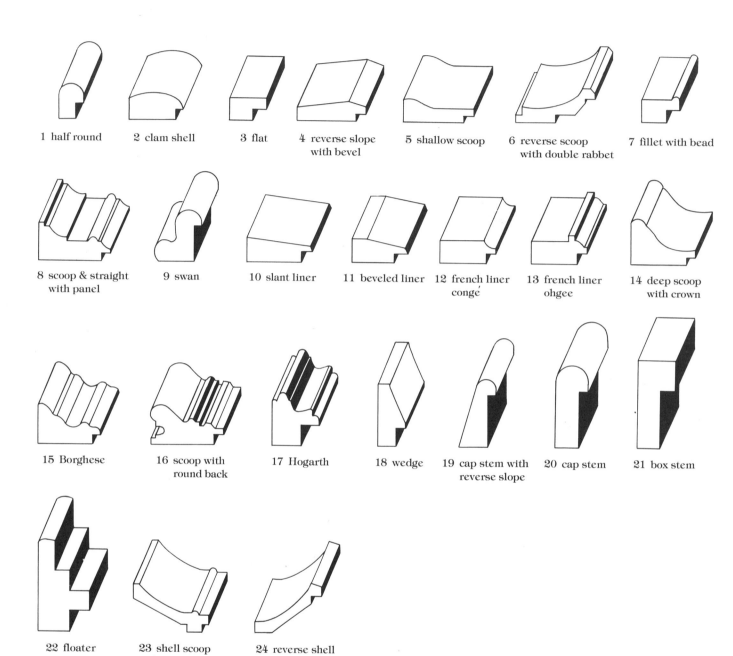

1 half round

2 clam shell

3 flat

4 reverse slope with bevel

5 shallow scoop

6 reverse scoop with double rabbet

7 fillet with bead

8 scoop & straight with panel

9 swan

10 slant liner

11 beveled liner

12 french liner congé

13 french liner ohgee

14 deep scoop with crown

15 Borghese

16 scoop with round back

17 Hogarth

18 wedge

19 cap stem with reverse slope

20 cap stem

21 box stem

22 floater

23 shell scoop

24 reverse shell

WOOD PROFILES

The mouldings pictured are the basic profiles of the industry. All companies will make them differently. Some will make them in different widths with several different finishes. Some will design their own and, of course, others may "borrow" a well designed moulding. The companies that actually design mouldings take into consideration the type of art that is in style, and make mouldings of various widths and colorations to suit.

There are trends in the framing industry just as there are in the decorating and clothing industries. Not only do the colors of moulding go out of style, the shapes do also.

Numbers 1, 2, and 3 are the most common of our mouldings. You will find these profiles available in various sizes from 1/2″ to 3″. The finishes could be almost anything from a coat of black spray paint to a 23 karat gold leaf.

Number 4, the reverse slope with bevel, is often used for contemporary art because of its sleek design. However, if it were a 1″ moulding it would suit a certificate.

Numbers 5, 7, 10, 11, 12 and 13 are used as mouldings and as liners. A liner is used in conjunction with other mouldings, such as combining number 12 with number 16. Number 7 is called a fillet (pronounced either fill ā′ or fill′ĕt). It will be available with and without a rabbet, and can be used within the rabbet of another frame or as a decorative lip under a mat.

Number 8 and number 15 are widely used in the industry. They will often have several panels of color along with accent lines in the small grooves. Number 17 is the Hogarth moulding, very popular with etchings because of its traditional black lacquer finish with gold beading accent on the top edge and lip. It is currently available in other finishes. Number 23 and 24 are trouble! They are difficult to cut and impossible to hold still in a vise. You will find this profile used often in ready-made frames.

Number 18, the wedge, is often used in shadow boxes in combination with a number 20, the cap stem. It can also be used alone. The wedge, also called the "shadow box" frame, was popular in the 50s for framing prints.

Numbers 19, 20, and 21 are stem mouldings and are often used for country and contemporary framing. Care should be taken when fitting this moulding. Because of the thinness of the wood and the depth of the rabbet you may need another support within the frame, depending on the weight of the artwork.

Number 22 is the floater — probably invented in New York City. It is for use with canvas paintings that have been stretched over wooden stretcher bars. The frame attaches to the backside of the painting so that it appears to float within the frame unit. The problem with this moulding is trying to combine 4 big sticks of moulding with 4 sides of a canvas painting and keeping all 8 sides aligned with one another.

FRAMES

Frames also have names. Most of the names are derived from the period frames. An unusual style called the spandrel is a frame made with a circle or oval opening within a square or rectangle. No matter how plain or fancy the design it is still a spandrel frame. There are, of course, triangle, octagon and hexagon frames — to name a few. What you need to know is that a frame is usually described by its inside opening design rather than its outside edge.

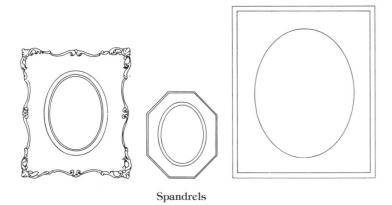

Spandrels

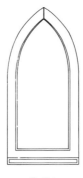

Gothic

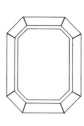

Octagon

CUTTING WOOD MOULDINGS

Wood moulding can be cut with a hand saw, electric saw, or chopper. Cuts must be clean and smooth, with no ragged edges on the top or bottom of the moulding. The most common cut for any square or rectangular frame is a 45° angle. No matter which equipment you choose, you will need to practice until you develop the right "feel" for cutting moulding. If you do not already have carpentry skills, you should probably spend some time developing them.

A miter box and hand-held backsaw are most often used by beginners. These are readily available from most lumber companies and hardware stores.

Electric saws are probably the most versatile cutters, because they will cut almost any wood and most soft metals. They are readily available and may already be a part of the framer's workshop. There are several models of electric saws available. The one pictured here is a "portable" model electric miter box with a special extension table for measuring moulding from the inside of the rabbet. You can also use an ordinary table saw with special adapters to control the angle of the cut. There are many saws made especially for this industry, which allow exact miter cuts. The "fastest cut in the land" can be made with an electric double-miter cut off saw.

The proper blade for your electric saw is usually available from machine manufacturers or suppliers. One that is recommended for cutting wood is an 80 tooth carbide-tipped blade with alternately beveled teeth. On this blade every other tooth is beveled at a 15° angle, with every fifth tooth cut straight across, acting as a "raker" to clean out the cut and make it smooth.

If you do not like working with saws, then the "chopper" is for you. It is an uncomplicated machine with two knives that work in a guillotine fashion. They are incredibly sharp and will slice through most woods with ease, leaving a very smooth cut. The machine may be manual or use "air", which means it is run by a compressor. A chopper has its limitations. It cannot cut very high or very wide scoop mouldings, and chopping hard woods can be a challenge. Under conditions of high humidity, the chopper can "crush down" a moulding that it would have cut very cleanly on a drier day.

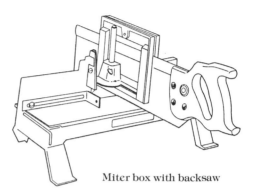
Miter box with backsaw

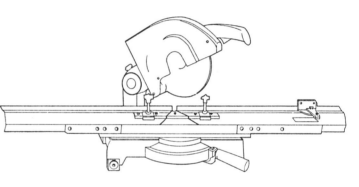
Electric miter saw

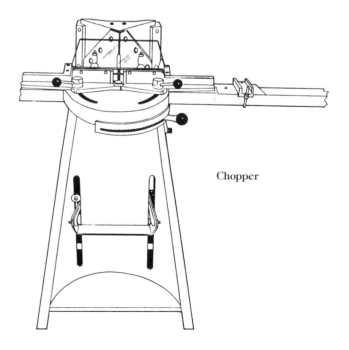
Chopper

JOINING WOOD MOULDINGS

To join wood in the traditional method you will need all the traditional tools of a carpenter: glue, nails, hammer, vise, and nail hole filler. GLUE should be a type used for woodworking. Most white glues dry brittle and are not waterproof. Titebond brand or comparable would be suitable. Hot melt glues are fast setting but a bit too thick for some small corners. The glue should not be visible in the finished corners. It needs to be thick enough to stick and stay but not so thick that it is "bulky". Because of wood's tendency to shrink as it ages, a combination of glue and nails is necessary to keep the corner from loosening.

NAILS

Wire nails, also called brads, are used to nail the mitered corner. Brads are nails with narrow heads. They are available in many lengths and thicknesses. You will need about 6 to 8 sizes. Buy these nails by the pound from our industry suppliers. They are usually not available in ordinary hardware stores.

One pound each of 6 to 8 sizes will give you a good selection. By the way, a pound of 1/2 x 20 will last your entire career in this industry — however, a pound of 3 x 12 will only give you about 60 nails. The larger the nail, the less of them in a pound.

Nails are measured by two sizes: length, which is in inches, and thickness, by gauge. Gauge runs backwards to what you may think — 20 is very thin and 12 is very thick.

Also available are cement-coated brads. These are used where extra strength is needed. The moisture in the wood "sets" the nail firmly.

You will need both glue and nails to hold the frame together.

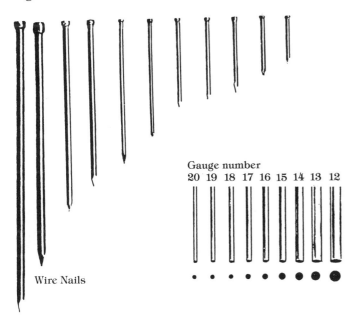

Wire Nails

Gauge number
20 19 18 17 16 15 14 13 12

HAMMER

You will need a lightweight hammer for this type of work. There are several weights to choose from. If you don't know what weight you prefer, go to a hardware store and hold several in your hand to get the proper weight. There are tack hammers, upholstery, claw and ball peen hammers. Buy a good quality, solid head, with a comfortable handle.

VISES

The 90° angle table vise is the most common vise. Even if you have other methods of joining, every shop should have at least one of these. They are available in cast iron or cast aluminum. Some have interchangeable plates to put in the center to change the joining angle from square to triangular, etc.

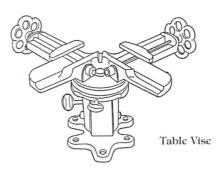

Table Vise

Some carpenters use a standard bench vise, which only holds one stick. You hold the other in place while nailing — it takes talent.

THE PROCESS

1) The vise should be attached to the work surface. It can be built into the table edge so that the arms of the vise are level with the table. That way the frame is supported while you are working on it.

   Take the two corners and place them into the vise. They should meet perfectly. If not, wiggle them and keep adjusting them until you get the right fit. There is no reason to make a frame with uneven miters or mismatched corners. If you cannot make the edges match, check the accuracy of the cut.

   If the miter has not been made correctly, you'll go crazy trying to make it fit. There is some amount of force that can be exerted when you fit it into the vise. If you force it too much, it will pop open later on. Some framers like to use a marker or ink dauber to color the inside cut on the miter so that any gap is less visible. However, if you have a good cut you should have little problem making a perfect corner.

2) Once you have your corner perfectly set you'll want to loosen the vise and pull out one side. Apply the glue and place back in the vise. Let the corner dry in the vise for 5-10 minutes, then move to the next corner. Excess glue will seep onto the finish of the frame. Glue will tarnish gold leaf. Wipe off excess glue completely.

3) Nailing the corners together will require planning. Try to make your nail holes neat and evenly placed. Note the four sketches depicting the different patterns you can use. A) This pattern is made by right-handed framers that do not turn the vise around. The opposite would be true of a left-handed framer. B) The nails are driven in the top and the bottom of the frame so they will be less obtrusive when the frame hangs on the wall. C) This pattern is for strength when building a large frame out of a stem moulding. D) This is cross nailing. Some framers think it adds strength, some think is messes up the corners too much.

Before pounding the nails into the moulding, you can drill the hole first. Drilling will give you a neat entry and lessen any problems with bent nails and missed hits. Drilling can be done with regular drill bits or you can use a nail with the head snipped off. Some softwoods do not require pre-drilling.

4) After hammering the nails into the wood use a nailset to push the nail in below the surface. Nailhole filler can be used to fill the hole. It comes in 30 or more colors and can be mixed to match color variations. To mix nailhole filler, take a bit of each color and put it onto a piece of plastic, fold over and squeeze the filler around until it mixes together.

If you missed the nail while hammering you probably created a halfmoon in the moulding. You can fix the dent with the use of a wet paper towel and tacking iron. Put a small piece of wet towel on the dent, place the heated tacking iron on the top of the towel — the dent should raise up. The combination of heat and moisture will expand the wood. This works great on moulding without gesso on it.

There are several other methods of joining using power hand tools such as staplers and nailers.

One of our industry's newest inventions is the v-nailer. This machine drives a v shaped blade into the underside of the frame. It is fast, easy, neat, strong, and best of all, no marred corners or nail hole filling. You can also assemble the entire frame and then set it aside to let the glue set up.

The v-nails are sharpened on one end to penetrate the wood neatly. There are several sizes available and some companies offer a special nail for oak and other hardwoods.

The v-nailer pictured is foot operated. When you step on the bar, the nail is forced up into the bottom of the frame corner. There are several machines on the market. Some are simple hand operated, one-nail-at-a-time, while others are available with power clamps, automatic gluing and power nailing.

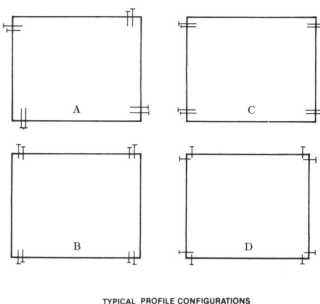

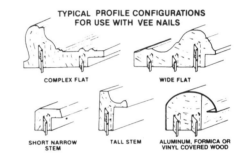

TYPICAL PROFILE CONFIGURATIONS
FOR USE WITH VEE NAILS

COMPLEX FLAT   WIDE FLAT

SHORT NARROW STEM   TALL STEM   ALUMINUM, FORMICA OR VINYL COVERED WOOD

(Backside Shown)

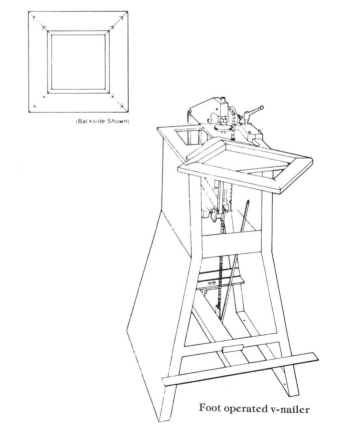

Foot operated v-nailer

METAL MOULDING

There are frames made of metals such as brass, copper and real silver but when picture framers speak of metal frames they mean extruded aluminum frames.

The first metal frames to reach public awareness were made in the late 1950s for the Museum of Modern Art in New York City. This was a welded corner design and was attached with screws to a strainer. This framing style is still used today although not as popular as the "metal section frame".

Metal sections are lengths of extruded aluminum moulding cut into pieces and fastened together with brackets in each corner. They became available in a pre-packaged kit form in 1968.

The most popular of the metal finishes is the silver or chrome finish followed by gold and black.

Aluminum moulding is colored by anodizing which produces a transparent, dye like coloring or by painting which produces a solid opaque finish. The painted finish has to be "baked" on to make it more durable.

The moulding can also be finished by different methods of polishing. The sides and top of the moulding can be "brushed" to give a little texture or high polished to make it smooth and shiny all over. Of course a combination of brushing and polishing give a different finish. A "frosted or matte" finish can be done to give a very soft look to the color and finish of the moulding.

There are different qualities of aluminum moulding just like there is in wood. A metal moulding manufacturer may be known for "high quality" or "promotional quality" moulding. You may find a more perfect finish on one brand or a thinner extrusion from another. Check the brands before choosing the one to suit your needs.

On the following page are just a few of the profiles available from the manufacturers of metal moulding. Each has been designed to serve various needs of the framer. The selection of styles as well as colors will change because of popularity of certain types of art as well as current color trends.

Profiles A,B,C,F and M will accommodate a canvas painting stretched over bars. A and M have a deep overhang of nearly 3/4 of an inch, which is especially good when you need room for expansion or error in measuring very large pieces. M is also used when extra strength is needed. It has an extra channel near the face of the frame to insert an extra set of hardware which will keep the corner tightly closed under extreme weight.

H has a narrow rabbet that works great when framing something "decorator style" between two pieces of glass.

J and L provide space between the artwork and the glass. You can use either for floating art or making a shadow box.

D is probably the all time most popular metal moulding. It is available in the most colors from almost any supplier and comes in length, chop or package kits.

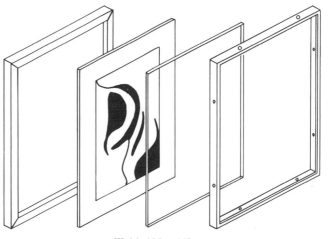

Welded Metal Frame

PROFILES OF METAL MOULDINGS

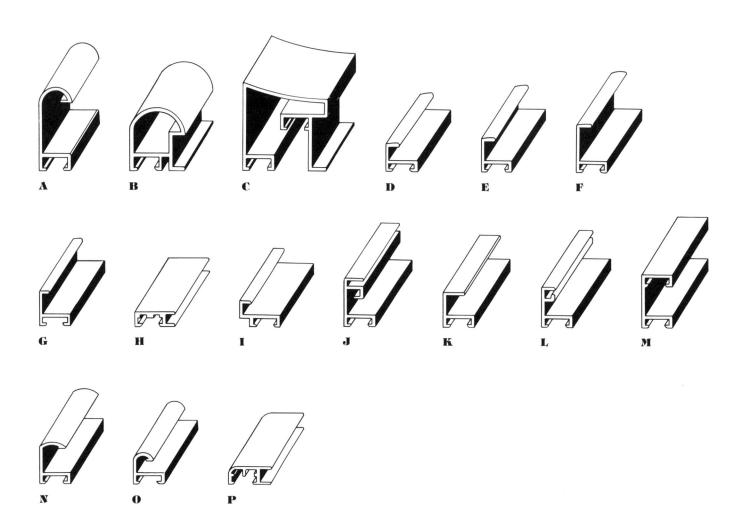

A B C D E F

G H I J K L M

N O P

WRAPPED MOULDINGS

This moulding is made by wrapping several types of pliable material over a wood core. The mouldings can be inexpensive or very expensive depending on the type of material used to wrap and the quality of the wood core to be wrapped. Wrapping materials used include: paper, vinyl, plastic, mylar, aluminum, brass and other metals. Joining should be done from the underside to prevent damage to the backside of the moulding. There are special matching nails available if you join in the traditional manner.

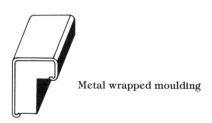

Metal wrapped moulding

CUTTING METAL MOULDINGS

An electric saw is necessary to cut metal moulding properly. It can not be cut on a chopper or with a hacksaw. If you use a hacksaw it will be a very rough cut. The saws pictured on this page are especially made to cut picture frame moulding. They will cut both wood and metal although the choice of blade will make a difference in the cut.

While surveying moulding manufacturers and framers, several recommendations were made for both blades and lubricants.

Choice of blades will vary according to the type of work you do as well as how much of it you do.

BLADES

Blades are available in several sizes (diameter) such as 10″, 12″ and 14″. The tooth on the blade is very important. The tooth can be a triple chip, which means that each tooth has a double bevel and a flat bottom. Or the tooth could have an alternate top bevel which means every other tooth is beveled at a 15° angle with every fifth tooth cut straight across which acts as a "raker" to clean out the cut. Or you could have the modified tooth style which has each tooth beveled at a 15° angle alternating left and right. How many teeth? Blades are sold, depending on diameter, with anywhere from 80 teeth to 200 teeth. The less teeth on a blade the faster it will get dull. A greater amount of teeth will help it last longer and give a good cut but will "load up" fast.

Blades are available in carbide or steel. The steel blade is for high volume and small shapes. You can feed the blade through the metal four or five times as fast as you would a carbide blade. You must use it fast because you don't want it to stay in the metal too long or it will get hot and load up. The carbide blade will last longer but cuts more slowly. The carbide blade would be the best choice if you are cutting both metal and wood on the same saw. When a blade is sharp you should not have to do any deburring. As the blade gets dull you may have to clean up the cuts with a file or a whetstone. The carbide blade should be used on any of the large metal profiles.

Blades must be lubricated to last and cut well. There are stick lubricants such as wax and animal fat, but they are not as efficient as a spray. On some model saws the lubricant is automatically applied. If you must apply your own, get a spray bottle and spray at least every other cut. Synthetic lubricants are very popular among the manufactures of both moulding and saws. The fluid should be available from the saw manufacturers.

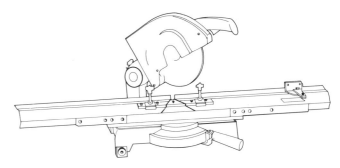

Electric miter saw

Double miter cutoff saw

ASSEMBLY OF A METAL SECTION FRAME

STEP 1 Clean work surface thoroughly. Bits of glass and wire or diamond points will scratch the moulding.
Lay out the frame sections face down.

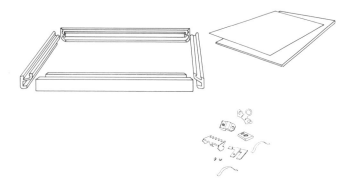

STEP 2 Insert two angles (some hardware systems may only have one) into the track at each end of the one side of the frame. Do not tighten screws, yet.

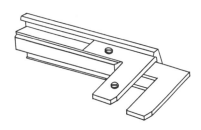

STEP 3 Slide each of the side pieces onto the exposed angles. Adjust each corner as you tighten the screws. It is possible to misalign the corners so that you can see daylight through the corners.

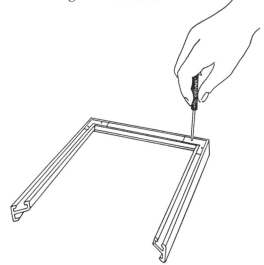

STEP 4 Slide the glass, mat, picture, backing etc. into the channel. If you are putting in a mounted poster with glass — careful glass doesn't slide on the face of the poster — it will slice off the printing!

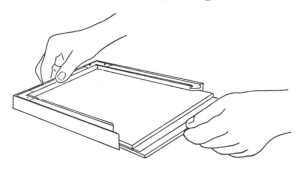

STEP 5 Insert the remaining corner angles into the remaining slide. Slide the exposed angles into the side pieces of the frame and tighten the four set screws.

Inspect the front to see that the corners are all lined up properly and check to make sure they are tight.

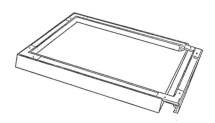

STEP 6 To tighten the contents within the frame you have several choices: a) Use the spring tension clips by pushing down on the arch of the clips and slipping them between the joining track and the backing. Caution: on large frames this method can cause boards and artwork to bow out. b) Filling the space with 1″ slices of foam center board — you may use double sided tape to hold them still. c) Filling in the space with boards the full size of the frame. Yes, it's more costly but you will not have the problems associated with the pressure from the spring clips.

STEP 7   Now we need to provide a hanger. There are several available. We will use 4 different styles.

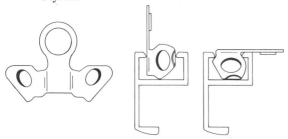

The SNAP HANGER has a simple snap-in making this hanger quick and easy to install. The hanger may be repositioned by pressing down with your thumb and sliding it up or down in the channel.

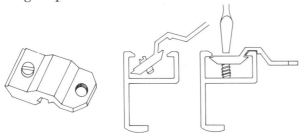

The SCREW HANGER is installed by tilting it so that it rests securely under the hardware channel lip. Once in position, tighten the screw until secure.

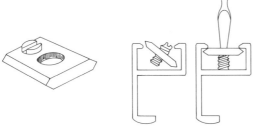

The RECESSED HANGER is designed to give less bulk for the hanging system and is easy to install by inserting it into the channel by tilting it. Once in position tighten the screw to secure it. The frame can then be hung by 2 hooks or nails or it can be wired. If you are wiring it, you may find putting the wire loosely through the holes before inserting the hanger into the frame will be easier than after they are in the channel.

The NOTCHED HANGER, very similar to the common sawtooth, has a unique snap in, snap out feature that makes for quick installation and removal. It can be positioned easily by sliding it in the channel.

STEP 8   When putting in your wire, wrap it around twice in the hanger, then wind it tightly to make it neat and clean. Neatly trim off excess wire.

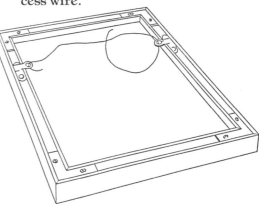

STEP 9   Put wall bumpers on the bottom edges and place your store label on the back.

25

PLASTIC MOULDINGS & FRAMES

Plastic box frames have become very popular for framing contemporary as well as antique pieces. It is often called a "no frame" frame. The plastic box frame, more properly called an acrylic box was initially designed to hold matted paper art. The attachment of the box to a wood strainer with screws allowed the depth to be adjusted to correctly accommodate the thickness of the artwork. Acrylic is also a good glazing because it allows a transfer of air to and from the art.

The deeper acrylic box can be used to hold thick art work, quilts or objects. The pieces can be attached to the support board that rests on the strainer. These boxes require specific skills to make. If you do not have these skills you can have the boxes made by someone that does.

Many framers are hesitant to work with acrylic because of its sensitivity to scratches. Acrylic sheets are usually covered with pressure-sensitive masking paper. This masking paper protects the surface from getting scratched in storage and handling. The surface hardness of acrylic is the same as copper or brass, so handle them with equal respect. The masking paper should not be removed until all machining and fitting operations are completed.

The masking paper can be removed by lifting each of the corners, one at a time, and peeling back paper towards the center of the sheet. If the sheet has been exposed to lots of sunlight, it will not come off unless you use naptha, or Solvesso-100 to moisten it. Any oily residue should be removed with soap and lukewarm water. Do not use benzene. If you intend to use the paper for re-masking, roll it around a cardboard tube as you pull it off the sheet of acrylic. Make sure to keep it very clean.

For normal fitting jobs, keep the masking paper on until the last minute. If the masking paper is removed carefully and slowly the sheet may be clean enough to be used without further cleaning. If there is a residue of masking adhesive use a soft cloth moistened in isopropyl alcohol, it evaporates quickly and does not leave any residue.

Acrylic boxes can also be cleaned with an anti-static cleaner which will reduce static electricity and dust attraction. It is applied by spraying or wiping with a soft cloth which has been dampened with the solution. Advice to your customers on the maintenance of the box is important. Tell them to use a very soft clean cloth with a solution of dishwashing liquid and water to clean the box or a commercial plastic cleaner. Have them understand they must never use paper towels — no matter how soft they feel — they are made of wood pulp and will leave tiny scratches. Never use solvents such as acetone, gasoline, benzene, carbon tetrachloride, lacquer thinner, window cleaning sprays or kitchen scouring compounds. Never use sharp instruments, scrapers or razor blades to remove spots.

Small scratches can be removed with toothpaste or with a polishing kit available from an acrylic supply company.

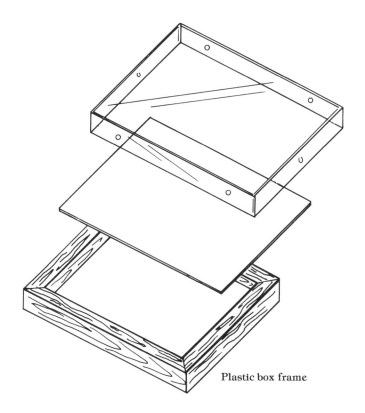

Plastic box frame

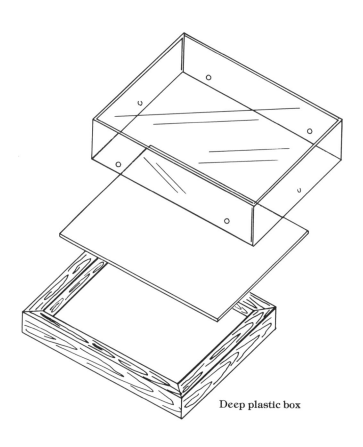

Deep plastic box

The simplified plastic box is less expensive than the other models because of the method of producing the acrylic. It is very easy to use. The back is made of cardboard and has several holes punched out in the back to facilitate the hanging of the box. It is made of a thinner plastic and is therefore very light weight. The plastic box just slips over the white cardboard inside box holding the artwork inside.

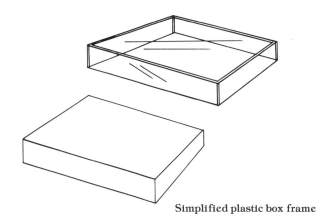

Simplified plastic box frame

Tenite is an economical moulding introduced in the early 1970s. This wood moulding has a plastic "cap" fitted into the top of the profile. The plastic cap is usually either gold or silver toned. The wood is stained or painted in many colors. The main drawback of the moulding is the "shrinking" of the plastic cap. Over a period of years, the plastic strip shrinks which opens the corner of the frame. It cannot be stretched out again. This moulding is available in length and ready-made frames.

Tenite moulding

Plastic section frames are now available in many profiles. Some of the profiles take metal corner brackets, similar to aluminum section frames, to secure them. The more economical profiles use snap clips, tape and glue to hold them together. The finishes often duplicate the metal frame finishes. A more recent design is available in clear plastic.

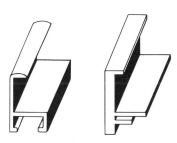

Plastic section moulding

Plastic laminated wood moulding is often called "mica" moulding. This wood core moulding is covered with a high gloss plastic laminate that gives a solid opaque finish that is available in many colors. As with other mouldings, there are different grades available. The poorer quality mouldings may blister, delaminate or warp. Some manufacturers have a matching nail hole filler for framers that join in the traditional manner using nails and glue. The perfect way to join this moulding is from the underside using a v-nailer or other type of concealed join.

Plastic laminated wood

MEASURING MOULDINGS

MEASURING MOULDING

Before ordering chop moulding, pricing a custom frame, or deciding whether you have enough moulding in stock for a particular frame, you must determine how much moulding will be required for the job. You need enough moulding to go all the way around the frame-ready artwork, including enough extra moulding to allow for the mitred corners.

Begin with the outside measurement you have figured for the artwork to be framed. Let's say, for example, that the measurement is 16″ × 20″. There will be two 16″ sides and two 20″ sides.

So:

$$16 + 16 = 32″ \qquad\qquad 16 + 20 = 36″$$
$$20 + 20 = 40″ \quad \text{or} \qquad\qquad \underline{\times\ 2}$$
then: $\qquad\qquad\qquad\qquad\qquad 72″$
$$32″ + 40″ = 72″$$

Now you have the running inches around the perimeter of the ready artwork. However you will need more inches to compensate for what will be cut away while making the mitre. Extra moulding is required for each of the mitred corners. Each square or rectangular frame will have four sides. Each side will have two 45° cuts. Each cut will require an additional "moulding width" of moulding. Measure across the width of the moulding, including the rabbet. Let's say our selected moulding is 1-1/2″ wide. Multiply 1-1/2″ × 8 mitre cuts to determine the quantity of additional moulding you will need. Add this total (12″) to the previous figure (72″); your grand total is 84″. Divide this final figure by 12 to translate inches into feet. It will take seven feet of this moulding to make your 16″ × 20″ frame.

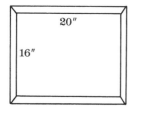
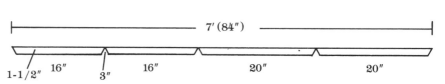

UNITED INCHES CHART

Moulding requirements may be quickly determined with the help of the "United Inches" chart. United inches refers to the united or combined inches of two sides of the frame. For the frame in our example, the united inches total is 16″ + 20″ = UI. Look on the side of the chart to locate 36 UI. The numbers to the right of the 36 refer to the footage required to make any frame that has the combined or united inches of 36. Depending on the width of the moulding the footage will be listed in thirds of a foot (4″). The chart has been prepared to compensate for the width of the moulding. For the 1-1/2″ moulding in our example, you will need seven feet of moulding to make the frame.

The next section to the right has the price per foot along the top. With the footage along the side. By cross-referencing the footage to the price you will arrive at the price of the frame.

Notice — round off figures upward when dealing with fractions. When working with the chart, round odd numbers upward to next even number.

United Inches	Width of Moulding					
	1	1½	2	2½	3	4
14	3	3⅓	3⅔	4	4⅓	5
16	3⅓	3⅔	4	4⅓	4⅔	5⅓
18	3⅔	4	4⅓	4⅔	5	5⅔
20	4	4⅓	4⅔	5	5⅓	6
22	4⅓	4⅔	5	5⅓	5⅔	6⅓
24	4⅔	5	5⅓	5⅔	6	6⅔
26	5	5⅓	5⅔	6	6⅓	7
28	5⅓	5⅔	6	6⅓	6⅔	7⅓
30	5⅔	6	6⅓	6⅔	7	7⅔
32	6	6⅓	6⅔	7	7⅓	8
34	6⅓	6⅔	7	7⅓	7⅔	8⅓
36	6⅔	7	7⅓	7⅔	8	8⅔
38	7	7⅓	7⅔	8	8⅓	9
40	7⅓	7⅔	8	8⅓	8⅔	9⅓
42	7⅔	8	8⅓	8⅔	9	9⅔

Number of Feet	3.00	3.25	3.50	3.75	4.00	4.25	4.50	4.75	5.00	5.50	6.00
4	12.00	13.00	14.00	15.00	16.00	17.00	18.00	19.00	20.00	22.00	24.00
4-1/3	13.00	14.05	15.15	16.25	17.30	18.40	19.50	20.55	21.65	23.80	26.00
4-2/3	14.00	15.15	16.35	17.50	18.65	19.85	21.00	22.15	23.30	25.65	28.00
5	15.00	16.25	17.50	18.75	20.00	21.25	22.50	23.75	25.00	27.50	30.00
5-1/3	16.00	17.30	18.65	20.00	21.30	22.65	24.00	25.30	26.65	29.30	32.00
5-2/3	17.00	18.40	19.85	21.25	22.65	24.10	25.50	26.90	28.30	31.15	34.00
6	18.00	19.50	21.00	22.50	24.00	25.50	27.00	28.50	30.00	33.00	36.00
6-1/3	19.00	20.55	22.15	23.75	25.30	26.90	28.50	30.05	31.65	34.80	38.00
6-2/3	20.00	21.65	23.35	25.00	26.65	28.35	30.00	31.65	33.30	36.65	40.00
7	21.00	22.75	24.50	26.25	28.00	29.75	31.50	33.25	35.00	38.50	42.00
7-1/3	22.00	23.80	25.65	27.50	29.30	31.15	33.00	34.80	36.65	40.30	44.00
7-2/3	23.00	24.90	26.85	28.75	30.65	32.60	34.50	36.40	38.30	42.15	46.00
8	24.00	26.00	28.00	30.00	32.00	34.00	36.00	38.00	40.00	44.00	48.00
8-1/3	25.00	27.05	29.15	31.25	33.30	35.40	37.50	39.55	41.65	45.80	50.00
8-2/3	26.00	28.15	30.35	32.50	34.65	36.85	39.00	41.15	43.30	47.65	52.00

Examples of working with the United Inch chart

Example A

Your customer brings in a needlepoint. She chooses a moulding 1″ wide. The blocked size of the needlepoint will be 12″ square. The moulding is $3.25 per ft.
1) add 12 + 12 = 24
2) Locate 24 on the UI chart
3) Cross over to 1″ width of moulding
4) It says that it takes 4-2/3 feet of 1″ moulding to make a 12″ square.
5) Locate 4-2/3 on the number of feet chart
6) cross over to the 3.25 heading
7) The cost of the frame is $15.15

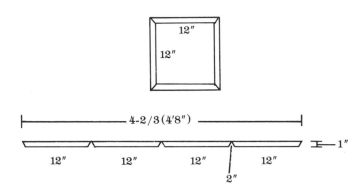

Example B

Your customer has chosen a 1-1/2″ bamboo moulding for a 12″ × 34″ frame. The moulding retails for $3.50 per ft.
1) Add 12 + 34 = 46 UI
2) Look for 46 and extend it to 1-1/2 for the moulding width = 8-2/3 ft. (8′8″)
3) Locate 8-2/3 on the next chart
4) Cross over to 3.50
5) The price will be $30.35

It will take 8′8″ of 1-1/2″ moulding to make a 12″ × 34″ frame. The retail cost of the frame is $30.35. This price is for the cut and joined empty frame. No glass, mats, or fit is included.

Example C

Your customer has chosen a 3/4″ moulding as a liner and a 2-1/4″ moulding as the frame. The liner sells for $2.00 per ft. and the frame for $3.00. per ft. The frame is a 18″ × 24″.
1) add 18 + 24 = 42
2) Locate 42 on the UI chart
3) cross over to the 3″ (the combined width of both mouldings) on the width chart
4) The answer is 9 feet. Locate 9 feet on the next chart under number of feet.
5) Cross over to the combined price of $5.00 per ft. The price of the cut and joined frame is $45.00.

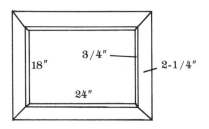

Example D

Your customer brings in an oil painting that is 24″ x 36″. She chooses a moulding that is 2-1/2″ wide at 5.50 per ft. You check the stock and find you only have two sticks, each 6′ (72″).
1) add 24 + 36 = 60 UI
2) Check 60 UI at 2-1/2 to find you need 11-2/3 ft.
3) 11-2/3 ft at $5.50 per ft = $64.15

Since you only have 4″ to spare on the amount of moulding in stock — take extra care when cutting.

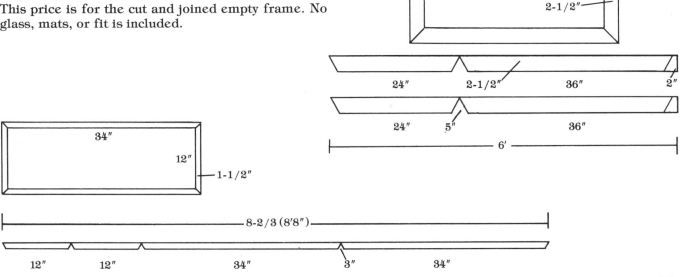

Glazing

GLASS

There are many kinds of glass. Picture framers are interested in flat glass. Flat glass can be classified as sheet, plate or float glass. Sheet glass is used for windows in homes. Plate and float glass are used where clear and accurate vision is needed. The terms "plate" and "float" describe the same type of glass. The float process for continuous production of flat glass was developed in England in 1959. Almost all flat glass produced today is float glass.

Clear glass is generally available in SSB grade. The SS stands for single strength or 2.5mm thickness. Picture strength glass is also available in some areas of the country. It is thinner - 2mm and harder, more brittle lite of glass, making it more difficult to cut and fit. Due to its thinness, large sizes may pose fitting and handling problems.

The "B" in SSB indicates window glass grade which allows a specified number of flaws known as seed, blisters, scratches, etc. Unfortunately, these flaws in the glass are highly visible in framing applications. Framers can expect these flaws unless the glass is specially processed.

Traditionally glass has been packaged in boxes of approximately 50 square feet, regardless of its weight or quality. There will be a different amount in each box, depending on the size lite you request. For example: a box of 16 x 20 contains 23 lites, while a box of 24 x 30 contains 10 lites, and a box of 11 x 14 contains 47 lites. Oversized glass may be packaged in half boxes or double boxes, depending on size and shipping requirements. You may notice some of the new specialty glasses being packaged in half boxes or other special cartons. Make sure you know how many lites you are getting for your money and price accordingly.

Lites of glass are protected from scratching each other by placing sheets of paper between each lite or by coating the lites with rosin. The rosin method is used for lesser quality glass, while paper sheeting is for the finer quality. It may cost you a few dollars more for the paper-sheeted variety, but it is much cleaner and easier to use. The money you save on paper towels, glass cleaner and labor will more than compensate for the few extra dollars that paper-sheeted costs.

CLEAR GLASS

Clear glass is available in many grades. The quality of clear glass will depend on the inspection process employed at each manufacture. Flaws, such as seeds, blisters, stones, cat-eyes and scratches may be considered normal by some manufacturers. Regular glass, as it is most often called, provides maximum clarity if produced as a quality product. When selecting clear glass, look for a premium grade. It may be time saving to have a glass that is polished, washed, inspected and packed with brown paper sheeting.

DOUBLE SIDED NON-GLARE

The first type of non-glare on the market was a double sided glass — meaning both surfaces of the glass were etched or patterned. Etching was accomplished by dipping the lite of clear glass in a hydrofloric acid solution causing a microscopic pattern on both sides of the lite. No acid remains on the glass, it is completely neutralized and removed. This treatment does break up the reflected light; however, it has a frosty appearance when distanced from the artwork. Most double-sided non-glare products offer a fine pattern that provides good glare control. Unfortunately, since both sides are etched the artwork is slightly diffused.

The patterned or rolled non-glare is made by pressing a pattern onto the surface of the glass while the lite is on the float line.

SINGLE SIDED GLARE CONTROL

This product was first introduced on the market in 1987, by Viratec as TruVue 2, later called Premium Non-Glare. This process etched only one side of the clear lite, thereby providing better resolution, less frost appearance and more light transmission.

Reflection Control Glass was introduced in 1989. It is made by the single side process however the resolution is superior to TruVue 2. Reflection Control allows viewing from a depth of three mats.

CONSERVATION GLASS

This is a new glass from Viratec TruVue that blocks 97% of the solar and artificial untraviolet light without altering the appearance of the glass. Conservation Glass is a high quality float glass which has a permanent layer of quartz bonded to one surface. This quartz glass-like material has the unique property of absorbing 97% of the ultraviolet portion of sunlight or fluorescent light. It is available in both clear glass with UV blocking and Reflection control with UV blocking. It cuts and cleans like regular glass.

MUSEUM GLASS

This is a new anti-reflective glass from TruVue. This product reduces overall reflection to less than 1%. Museum glass blocks 97% of the UV light while offering a high light transmission of 95%. The coating is softer than the surface of clear glass but harder than plastics or Denglas. Museum glass permits the highest light transmission, the least reflections, UV protection and is simple to cut and clean.

DENGLAS

This is the best known anti-reflective glass in the industry. Made by Denton Vacuum, it offers maximum light transmission with minimum light reflection. Denglas reduces overall visible light reflection from 8% to 1%. It is treated on both sides with special coating which permits 95% of the available light to be transmitted through the glass allowing for reflection free viewing. Both surfaces have a multilayer optical coating similar to that on fine camera lenses. The coating is chemically neutral and cannot affect artwork. Denglas can be used in shadow boxes of any depth. The surface is more difficult to clean and may require a special cleaner for efficiency. The coating may have a hint of purple or green, depending on the production lot.

HOW TO CUT GLASS

HOW TO CUT GLASS BY HAND
1) Set the lite of glass down onto a clean work surface. Any bits of glass, wire or a diamond point will scratch the glass. If you clean the glass before cutting your cutter will last longer and your cut will be smoother.
2) Hold the glass cutter so that it's comfortable in your hand when you draw it towards you. Position the head of the cutter so the wheel is straight up and down — not at an angle to the glass. Use a T-square as a guide for the cutter. Apply as much force as you need to get a score but not to crush the glass. If you are getting a lot of white bits, you are pushing too hard. Keep the pressure as even as you can, and run off the edge of the glass.
   Do not retrace a cut or try to connect the skips — it ruins the head of the cutter and is unnecessary.
3) Once the score has been made, take the odd edge of the glass to the edge of the table and snap it off. If it will not snap off, use the ball end of the cutter to "run the score" and the piece will just fall off.
4) There are glass pliers available that have a special grip within the jaws to break off the glass. Should you leave a small bit of glass attached that you wanted off — use one of the three notches just above the cutting wheel. Use the handle as a lever and take a "bite" of the glass to break it off.

2

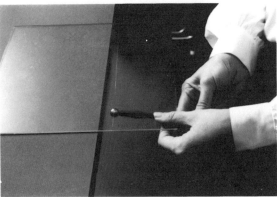

3

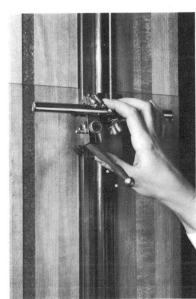

1

HOW TO CUT GLASS BY MACHINE
1) Slide lite of glass into place. Insert the glass cutter head in the slot so it reaches into the cut out area on the base board. Secure the cutter with a turn screw.
2) Glide the cutter over the glass, once only. Open the cutter and slide the glass to the right and break off excess.
Note: with the cutter in the slot it will cut the glass 1/8″ smaller than you measured on the extension arm. So adjust for it by extending the lite 1/8″. All parts that fit into the frame should be the same size. The frame should be 1/8″ larger than all the materials to allow for expansion.

2

HOW TO CUT OVAL GLASS

CUTTING AN OVAL GLASS WITH A HAND HELD CUTTER

Use this method for any size ovals, fan shape, or any weird size frame you have to fit.

1) Place the frame on top of a piece of glass. Use a permanent marker or grease pencil to trace the shape of the inside of the rabbet.

2) The framer here is using two hands to hold the cutter — you can use whatever grip gives you the most control. You also may need a low table so that you can lean over it while you are cutting. Score the glass — do not press so hard on the cutter that you leave a trail of white bits — use a light touch to score. Go completely around the oval — do not over cut — it will ruin the cutter blade. If you skip once in a while, let it go, it will connect later.

3) Score lines out to the edge. Start 1/8″ from the edge of the oval. Make several cuts like a star burst. The glass may fall away at this time. If not...

4) Pick up the glass and rap one of the score lines with the ball end of the cutter. This action will "run the score".

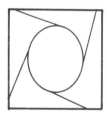

GLASS CUTTERS

Cutters used for glass can range from the basic hand held type to the wall mounted dual post style. There are several varieties of cutters available. The hand held models may have self oiling features or diamond heads instead of carbide wheels. Cutters will last longer if they are lubricated. Glass companies will tell you to set them in a small container of light oil — it's a great idea but messy in the framing room. Instead you might put a sponge loaded with light oil in that small container. This way the wheel will be resting in the oil but not soaked.

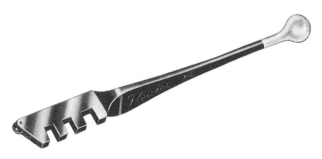

This is the most common glass cutter and the most useful. It is available with steel or carbide wheels. The ball on the top of the handle is used to rap on the glass to "run the score". The three notches just above the wheel can break off shards or bits of glass.

1

2

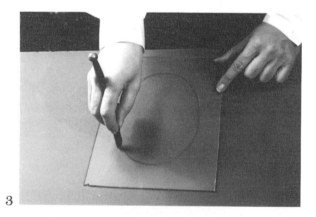

3

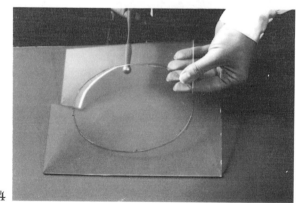

4

5) If you are left with a little piece still attached where you don't want it, you can break it off with one of the slots on the head of the glass cutter. Notice the slots are three different sizes and will take different "bites" out of the glass.

6) When the job is complete you should have all the parts broken away and be left with a useable oval.

5

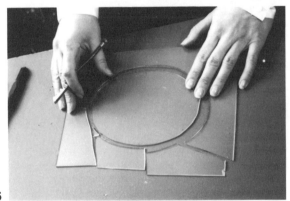

6

CUTTING GLASS ON AN OVAL MACHINE
1) Most oval/circle board cutters will also cut glass. You will have to change the board knife to a glass cutter. Set your measurements the same as you would for cutting a mat board. In this case the measurements are the inside dimension of the rabbet in the frame.
2) Center the piece of glass. You can use the hold down bars or even a piece of double sided tape to hold the glass in place.
3) Put both hands on the knobs and apply pressure on the cutter 'til it contacts the glass. Hold the pressure as evenly as possible and score around the shape. Do not score twice or let your cutter go over the line — even a little bit — it ruins the cutters. If you get lots of white bits of glass — you are pushing down on the cutter too hard. A score is a light touch.
4) After the score, take the glass out, turn it over on a flat surface and press the score line all the way around with your thumb. You will see the score "run". Interruptions in the cut will go together as it runs.
5) While the glass is still face down, take a hand held cutter and cut a star burst pattern. If the glass does not break away — use the ball at the end of the cutter and rap the glass with it — the pieces will break off.

PLASTIC GLAZING

There are several names framers will call this type of glazing. Plexiglas, a trade name of Rohm & Haas has become the "Kleenex" name in the industry. Plexiglas is an acrylic sheet, however there are other brands and many types of plastics other than acrylic used.

There are two types of plastics that framers are likely to deal with: styrene and acrylic. Plastics are limited in use as framing materials because they scratch easily, and because they should not be used over loose media such as pastels and charcoals. Care must be taken when cleaning plastics they are susceptible to scratching. Plastics are useful when shipping because of their light weight. They are available in 1/8″, 1/4″, and regular and non-glare finishes.

STYRENE is a very economical plastic sheeting found in craft and art supply stores. You can identify styrene by its green or clear plastic protective wrapping. Styrene yellows as it ages. The discoloration is activated by heat. There is one type of styrene that is available that will filter 70 to 85% of the UV light. Styrene is usually quite thin (.040″) therefore you are limited to smaller sizes that will stay upright and rigid in the frame job. This product is not recommended for professional framers.

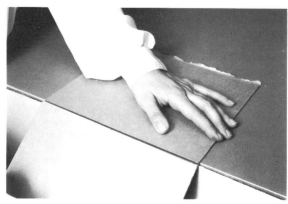

ACRYLIC is preferred by professional framers because of its clarity, strength and resistance to discoloration. Acrylic is also available with ultraviolet filtering ability. It is graded from one to five. UV-3 will give protection for conservation purposes. Acrylic is identified by its coated brown paper wrapping.

Plastics are available in clear and non-glare; the clear is usable, but the non-glare variety is often too cloudy. Remember acrylic or styrene must not be used on loose art media because static electricity may cause the media to lift and transfer to the glazing.

CLEANING

Do not use ordinary cleaning agents on plastics. They ruin the polished finish of the plastic. Use water with a little bit of Lux liquid (or equivalent) mixed in. Apply with a soft cloth. No scratchy paper towels, please. There are also plastic cleaners available that control the static that develops while working on the plastic. You can buy kits that will remove scratches from plastic. They are available at craft stores and glass stores. They will sand the surface and then buff it to its original sheen.

CUTTING

Acrylic will come with a cover sheet on each side to protect it while handling. The paper sheet can be left on while you are cutting it. You can cut acrylic with a hand-held cutter, similar to a linoleum knife, or use a wall mounted cardboard and glass cutter.

You can also use electric saws, such as a table saw, a radial arm or even a jigsaw to cut the plastic sheet.

When cutting the plastic with a hand tool, you will be dragging the cutter through the plastic, cutting a groove in the sheet. After two or three slices into the sheet, take it to the edge of the table and bend the cut off area until it snaps off. You can also use glass pliers to bend and break the cut.

4

Paper and Boards

Paper and boards: two important daily tools of the framing trade. Every day you will look at them, handle them, confer with customers about them, and make decisions concerning them. About 90% of the artwork that you frame will be done on paper, and almost all of the framing you do will require matting, mounting, and filler boards to some degree. Understanding the nature of these materials and learning to identify them improves the quality of service you can provide in your shop. Although the subject is complex and involved, a working knowledge of the basics is all you really need. Let's begin at the beginning.

In the early days of writing, the search for a portable writing surface included tablets of stone, clay, wood, metal, and bone. The first truly practical surface was devised by the Egyptians over 4,000 years ago. It was made from a lattice-weave of wet reeds, pounded, pressed and air-dried. It was called "papyrus," a Greek word meaning "reed." Although it was not true paper, it is from the word "papyrus" that our word "paper" was derived.

It is generally believed that the first true paper was made in China in 105 A.D. by a court official named Ts'ai Lun. It was probably created in an effort to provide a writing surface that was cheaper than silk and less cumbersome than wooden tablets, but it had to be smooth enough to hold fluid calligraphy brush-strokes. Ts'ai Lun's paper was most likely made from silk scraps, hemp, and mulberry bark, mixed with water and mashed into pulp. After the water was pressed out, the thin mat of fibers was hung to dry. Despite centuries of innovation and automation, this is still the essential process of papermaking.

The Chinese closely guarded the secret of paper-making for several hundred years. In 751 A.D., Arabs in Central Asia successfully repelled a Chinese invasion; expert papermakers were among their Chinese prisoners. The art of papermaking spread quickly and widely throughout the Middle East and into Europe, where skin parchment had been the usual writing surface. Because the Chinese materials were not readily available in the West, fibers from the plentiful flax plants (used to make linen) were substituted, and eventually cloth fibers became the standard in paper-making. Many centuries passed before technology brought wood fibers back into popular Western use.

During the first Industrial Revolution (mid 1400s), there were many advances in automation, and many machines were created to improve papermaking. Even so, it remained a slow, tedious process, and the paper produced was expensive. Because paper was in small demand, there was plenty available to those who required it.

Papyrus

Oriental papermaking

The invention in 1450 of the Guttenberg movable-type press caused an enormous increase in the need for paper for printing. Papermaking still suffered from slow production techniques and a shortage of materials, so technology sought solutions, most of them at the expense of quality of the paper.

The Hollander machine (1680) greatly increased the speed of the pulping process. It used high-speed metal blades to blend rags with water, so that even the toughest rags could be reduced to a smooth pulp. The Hollander produced shorter fibers than those made by the old stamping technique that used pounding hammers, and these fibers produced a weaker paper. Still, the Hollander could make 50-100 times more pulp than the hammers!

Hollander

There were experiments with "sizing" (dipping paper into tubs of gelatin made from animal hoofs, horns and hides) to make a "harder" paper surface for the ink from stiff quill pens, which tended to bleed and feather. Sizing helped paper to compete with smooth parchment, and it quickly became a standard procedure. It was later discovered that adding alum (aluminum sulphate) to the gelatin size helped it to harden and prevented it from spoiling in the tubs. Alum soon became a standard material of papermaking, and it is still used today. Unfortunately, it greatly increases the acidity of the paper produced, severely reducing its strength and permanence.

There were also experiments with bleaching, to whiten paper made from stained or colored rags. Chlorine was discovered in 1774, and was used in papermaking in 1792. The terrible results were quickly evident — the paper deteriorated so rapidly that some book pages crumbled to dust before they could even be bound!

In 1798, Frenchman Nicholas Louis Robert developed a papermaking machine that revolutionized the industry. It was patented by the Fourdrinier brothers in London and called the Fourdrinier machine. Paper was formed on a continuous, wire mesh belt, which shook from side to side (causing fibers to interlock) as it carried the pulp mixture to pressing rolls, where most of the water was expelled. Then, the continuous roll of paper was wound through heated cylinders to complete the drying process. This machine allowed true mass production. For the first time, writing paper and books were affordable to the average person.

Sorting cotton scraps

The need for cloth fibers became greater than ever. Eli Whitney's cotton gin (1793) helped by increasing the supply of cotton linter (the short fuzz that clings to cotton seeds after the first ginning). Still, supply struggled to keep up with demand, and the cost of raw materials remained high.

The search for a cheaper substitute for rags prompted experiments with a variety of plant fiber sources, including potatoes, cattails, and cornhusks, but wood seemed to show the most promise.

In 1840, a German named Friedrich Keller invented a grinder that reduced logs to wood pulp, and in 1865, American chemist C.B. Tilghman discovered a process that used sulfurous acid to dissolve the ground wood, leaving fibers suitable for papermaking. After an absence of a thousand years, wood pulp was welcomed back to Western papermaking as a cheap and plentiful source of pulp.

Today there are 7,000 different types of paper catalogued, but all of them are made with some system of these basic steps: pulping, forming, couching (laying down), pressing, and drying. The three major techniques of modern papermaking are handmade, moldmade, and machinemade.

HANDMADE PAPERS are generally more interesting and attractive than those made by the other methods. Each sheet is made individually, using a hand mold. Hand papermaking is a skilled craft, and every sheet is a work of art.

Handmade papers are usually made from cotton or oriental fibers, seldom from common wood pulp. Because they are formed more slowly than other types of paper, the fibers have more time to interlock, producing a very strong sheet.

The hand mold consists of a "deckle" (an outer rim that surrounds the mold), and a frame on which rests a brass wire mesh. The thickness and spacing of the wires partly determine the surface texture of the paper produced. The mold is dipped into the pulp mixture, then shaken to even out the mixture and remove excess pulp. The deckle prevents most of the pulp from running over the edges, but does allow some to spill over, creating feathery "deckled" edges on the paper. Handmade papers have no true grain, because the mold is shaken in both directions and the fibers intertwine both ways. Each sheet is laid down (couched) individually between two pieces of felt, then a layered stack of paper and felt is pressed to remove moisture. This produces sheets of paper with nearly identical front and back surfaces.

Handmade papers often feature "watermarks," which are symbols of the papermaker. They are sewn into the wire mold with brass wire. When the mold is shaken from side to side less pulp forms on the sewn area, thus, creating a somewhat transparent mark.

The size of handmade paper is limited by the dimensions of the mold one worker can handle. This has usually been about 22" x 30", although larger sizes have appeared in recent years, sometimes requiring two people to dip and shake one mold.

Making handmade paper

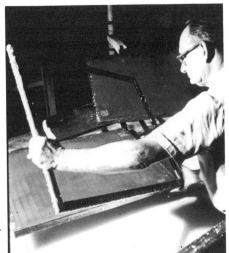

Deckle and mold
for handmade paper

Examples of watermarks

MOLDMADE PAPERS are made on a small machine in which the hand mold is replaced by a rotating cylinder. The cylinder picks up pulp from a rotating vat and releases it onto a moving felt. Moldmade papers have some grain direction, but less than papers made by Fourdrinier machines, because the cylinder mold moves slowly enough to allow some interlocking in both directions. As with handmade papers, this increases the strength of the sheet. The tight, uniform formation provided by the cylinder gives more consistent thickness from sheet to sheet than is possible with handmade papers.

Moldmade papers have two natural and two "interior" deckles. The artificial deckles are made by a wire seam called a "waterline," along which the wet sheets are torn to separate them. Although most moldmade papers consist of all cotton fibers, some are only half cotton and half high-quality wood pulp. Moldmade papers may have watermarks produced like those in handmade paper. And, also like handmade, moldmade papers are generally white, off-white, or cream, with no whiteners or dyes added, in an effort to keep the finished product non-acidic. In recent times, some non-acidic dyes have been developed and are used occasionally.

Moldmade papers are produced in rolls, and can be made in a wide variety of weights and sizes. Because of the time involved in production, and the quality of materials, both handmade and moldmade papers tend to be significantly more expensive than machinemade papers.

MACHINEMADE PAPERS include all of the many varieties produced by Fourdrinier-type machines. These papers are mass produced on conveyor belt production systems that begin with a "wet end" (pulp/water blending) and finish with completed rolls of paper at the "dry end." Machinemade papers may be thin or thick, smooth or rough, white or colored, and can be produced in many weights and sizes.

Machinemade papers have a wire side (the side of the sheet in contact with the wire mesh conveyor belt), and a "felt" side (created when the pulp/water mixture passes through rollers covered with heavy, absorbent felt or synthetic blankets). These two surfaces are also called "right side" (wire) and "wrong side" (felt).

Machinemade papers may be made from many types of fibers, including cotton, wood, and even synthetics. Machinemade papers have a grain, created as the pulp mixture on the belt is shaken from side to side, entwining fibers and settling the pulp to an even thickness.

A machinemade paper can have a deckled edge made by a deckle-strap extended across the wire, or by jets of air or water along the conveyor belt route,

causing interruptions in the sheet at specified points. Machinemade papers can also have a watermark, produced by a "dandyroll" — a cylinder that rolls across the paper, imprinting watermarks. Many surface finishes are made by rolling paper through cylinders, such as the heavy "calenders" that make smooth surfaces.

Sizing, usually a solution of glue, starch, or resins, is used on all but blotter-type papers, to close up the pores of the paper and reduce absorbency. Sizing is usually done by dipping papers into the solution, coating the finished surface.

BOARDS begin with plys (layers) of paper, glued together and pressed until they form a sheet of the desired strength and thickness. Rolls of paper are fused into boards on a machine called a "paster."

Most boards consist of a cover sheet, core, and backing sheet. However, a few types of board (such as chipboard and ragboard) are not made from plys of paper, but are thick sheets of pressed pulp.

Boards are produced in a range of standard sizes. They are cut to size automatically as they emerge from the pasting machine. The quality of boards varies greatly, and depends upon the quality of the paper layers or pulp they are made from.

Modern papermaking

TYPES OF BOARDS

Boards are simply layers of paper pasted or laminated together to form a sheet. The thickness is measured in points or plys. Most often framers will use plys to describe the thickness of boards. Not all boards are made of paper nor are they all in plys, yet this term will describe the relative thickness.

Many boards will be measured with the following designations:

ST	single thick	approx.	1/16"	14 ply	40 pt.
DT	double thick	approx.	1/8"	28 ply	80 pt.
TT	triple thick	approx.	3/16"	42 ply	120 pt.

Some boards are formed, that is they are made of a solid mass rather than layers of paper. For the sake of reference they are still referred to in plys, to help you judge their thickness.

CORRUGATED BOARD

The most common, yet the worst board to be near artwork. It is made of kraft paper laminated on each side of a kraft fluted middle. It can be very strong and ridged, yet deadly to artwork because of its high acid content. It will damage work that is near it and leave brown lines that are not removable. If you use this as a filler board keep it well away from the item being framed. It should not be used for conservation framing at all.

Magnified profile of corrugated board

CORRUGATED ACID-FREE

Is constructed the same as kraft paper, except the materials used in the manufacture have been treated to render them acid-free. It makes an excellent filler board for conservation framing.

NEWSBOARD/CHIPBOARD

Chipboard is brownish in color while newsboard is grayish brown. Each is composed of recycled materials. This solid-core board is very dense and ridged but highly acidic. It can be used as a filler or support board but should not be in direct contact with the art. Because it contains uncontrolled recycled materials it is a risky board to use for any adhesive mounting. Some areas may resist or repel the adhesive. This board holds staples and tacks very well. Upson board is a trade name for this type of thick board.

Magnified profile of news board

REGULAR MOUNTING BOARDS

Regular mounting boards are not acid-free but they may be useful in certain situations. 12C is an extremely thick, 3/16 inch, newsboard, It is very strong and dense. It will accept staples and pins. X is single thick while 3X is double thick. They both have a smooth finish with white acid-neutral surface paper on both sides.

Magnified profile of mounting board

ACID-FREE MOUNTING BOARDS

These boards are double sided white acid-free mounting boards. The core as well as the surface papers are acid-free. They are available in several thicknesses. AFX is a single thick board while AF3X is double thick. 11W is a new needlework board that is white on both sides and has an acid-free core as well as face sheets it is extra thick — 3/16 inch.

POSTER BOARD

There are several types of poster board. They are not used for matting purposes. The better quality has a news middle with a non-bleeding, non-fading laminated coated surface paper designed to accept mediums of sign painters and screen painters. There is a craft poster board that has a very sensitive coating. It will smear, watermark and fade.

Magnified profile of poster board

FOAM CENTER BOARD

Inert white plastic center faced on both sides with white sheeting. Although generally safe to use near artwork, if exposed to a great deal of light it will discolor. It is available in 1/8″, 3/16″ and 1/2″ thick and in sizes up to 4′ X 8′ Avoid the type made from thousands of tiny beads sandwiched between two layers of paper it is not solid and will crumble when cut. It also softens in the dry mount press and will leave bumps and dents.

Magnified profile of foam center board

ACID FREE FOAM CENTER BOARD

Inert white plastic center faced on both sides with acid-free paper.

STANDARD MAT BOARD

The quality of the mat board is judged by the center core, what it's made of and how it is processed Standard mat board has an unbuffered groundwood pulp center. Untreated groundwood is highly acidic and will discolor and deteriorate over a period of time. The same will happen to the artwork it houses.

Magnified profile of standard mat board

ACID FREE REGULAR MAT BOARD

This is standard 14 ply mat board, that has been buffered. The center core and the backing paper have been treated with calcium carbonate to a neutral pH level. This board could be used where color and high permanence are important, but the artwork is decorative.

SULFITE BOARD

Chemical wood pulp center which has been treated to purify it. The purest form of Sulfite, "Alpha Pulp", comes closest to matching the natural purity of cotton cellulose. It is acid-free with buffered cover papers.

Magnified profile of sulfite board

RAG MAT

This "top of the line" board is made of 100% cotton fibers and is a pure natural fiber. It should have a neutral pH. It has short and long fibers. Short fibers cut easier and the long fibers require less processing, cooking, bleaching, beating, and washing so they remain longer and stronger and by nature are more durable. It is also neutral sized (buffered) for added longevity. If surface paper colors are added to the face of the board they would be acid-free also. Solid colors are available but in very limited selection because of the requirements of the coloring agents to be acid-free. Rag mat can be used on any item you frame or mount with complete confidence of its museum quality.

Magnified profile of rag board

ARCHIVAL PHOTO MOUNT BOARD

This board is especially made for photographs and artwork requiring a non-alkaline environment. It is a 4-ply, 100% cotton rag with a solid color throughout.

CUTTING AND TRIMMING boards can be done with a utility knife and a good ruler or you can use one of the machines illustrated here. The wall mounted cardboard and glass cutter reduces the risk of unsquare boards and glass. It is very simple to operate and has a special head on it that will accept a glass cutter or razor blade. The measuring rule sticks out to the left of the machine. This will move out of alignment if not protected from people using it as a support system. Square it up often. There are several brands of this machine — some are stronger than others. It is a machine you will use constantly. It will cut newsboard, mat board and foam centered boards as well as glass.

The next machine is a paper cutter. Many framers have been cutting mat board and mounting boards on this machine. It was not meant to cut boards and will fight the effort, however you can cut boards on it. The cutter will wear out faster and require blade sharpening and also a very firm grip on the part of the framer doing the cutting. They are available in several sizes — the 3' square is the most useful to a frame shop. The third cutter on this page is a table model board cutter. It has been designed to cut thick boards accurately. It is, of course, more expensive, than the paper cutter.

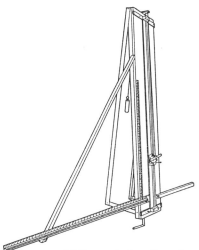

Wall mounted cardboard and glass cutter

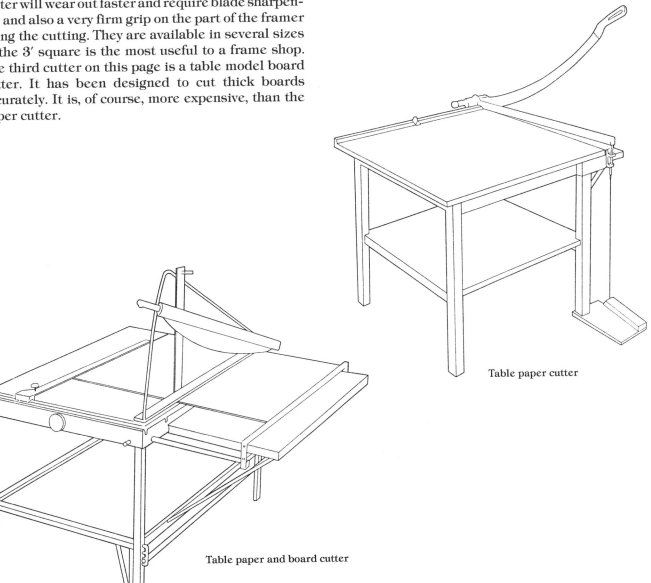

Table paper cutter

Table paper and board cutter

STORING MAT BOARDS is simple. You can build or buy double stack racks like the one pictured, or you can build slots under your framing tables. Since most mat boards measure 32″ x 40″ you will need a minimum clearance of 34″ x 42″. Although racks can be used either vertically or horizontally, it is easier to retrieve a mat board from a "packed" vertical rack than a "packed" horizontal rack.

HINT: When your boards get scuffed from brushing against each other, dampen a clean sponge with clear water and wipe over the scuff. The water will raise the fibers that were smashed down. This will also clean up a dusty board.

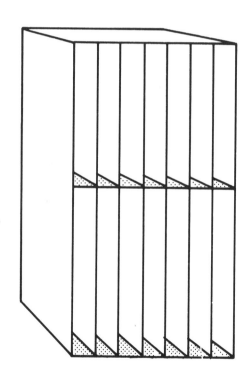

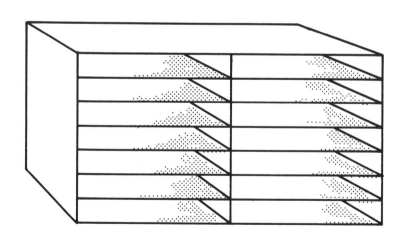

QUALITY & PERMANENCE

Papers are made for many purposes. Boards are made from layers of paper. The materials in manufacturing are chosen with the end use of the paper in mind. Let's examine the factors that determine the quality and performance of paper and boards.

The increasingly acidic chemical composition of our environment poses a great threat to paper. Acid slowly destroys the molecular structure of paper. Eliminating the acid content in paper is a primary goal when producing an "archival" paper, meaning the paper satisfies museum conservation standards. The acid quality of paper is determined by a number of factors during production.

Regardless of technique, it takes about 99 lbs. of water to make one pound of paper, and even after the final pressing and drying, paper still contains about 5-6% water. So the quality of the water makes a difference.

Very few paper mills are situated near the limestone rich underground reservoirs that provide the best acid-neutral water naturally. So most mills, whose water is supplied typically by a nearby lake or river, use chemical purification to remove acidic pollutants.

Alum (aluminum sulphate) is commonly used in modern papermaking. It is called "the papermaker's helper" because it alters the state of water so that pulp fibers form sheets better and faster. It also helps fix colors and other additives to the fibers. Unfortunately, alum reacts with moisture and impurities in the atmosphere, increasing acidity and causing deterioration of the strength and permanence of the paper. The highest quality papers must be made with no alum used in any stage of production.

The fiber content of the pulp base is an essential factor in determining quality. The fibers used in papermaking come from plants, all of which are made up mostly of various types of cellulose.

The type called "alpha cellulose" displays the greatest permanence. While it is possible to refine the alpha cellulose content in many plants (even wood) until it reaches archival standards, cotton is at least 93% alpha cellulose in its natural form. Therefore, cotton fibers are commonly preferred in making fine quality papers.

Most non-archival papers contain chemical brighteners to enhance their appearance. These additives do not meet archival standards, and must not be used in a paper designed for permanence.

The term Neutral pH (NpH) is a statistical measurement of the acid or alkali content in paper.

The desirable "neutral level" falls midway on the scale of 0 to 14 used for measuring. At pH7 a substance is neither acidic nor alkaline. Below pH7 a substance is acidic, and above 7 it is alkaline. A paper may be naturally neutral, or chemically balanced, meaning the acid present in the paper has been artificially neutralized.

Although papers may be acid-free and NpH when produced, they are susceptible to acid in the environment after production.

Buffering compounds such as calcium carbonate are added to high quality papers to protect them from damage caused by our acidic atmosphere. Small amounts (2-3%) of these buffering compounds are added to the pulp. The compounds will combine chemically with acids, providing a shield against deterioration and maintaining a satisfactory neutral pH level. This shield is called the Alkali Reserve.

Although most paper art generally prefers an alkaline environment, it has recently been discovered that some types of photographs have a chemical reaction to an excessive alkaline environment. Therefore when matting or mounting photographs it would be safer to use a rag mat specifically made for this purpose such as Photo Mount Rag mat which is 4ply, pH neutral, 100% cotton board.

Taking all of these elements into consideration, the finest, most durable papers and boards should be acid and alum free, made entirely of cotton (rag) or alpha cellulose fibers, and buffered against environmental impurities.

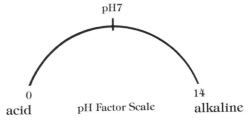

pH7

0   14
acid   pH Factor Scale   alkaline

ART PAPERS

The following is a list of papers and related terms you may encounter as a picture framer.

COATED

Paper treated with clay to make it smooth and opaque. Excellent for commercial printing. Often used for posters and reproductions. Varnished and laquered papers are also called "coated".

CHARCOAL/PASTEL PAPER

Either a white or colored drawing paper with a texture or "tooth" that holds the chalk or pastel onto the paper.

CONSTRUCTION PAPER

Available in many colors. Used by school children. Very poor quality paper that fades fast and becomes brittle.

COLD PRESS

A medium, slightly toothy finish on paper or boards. Also called Kid or Vellum finish.

DECKLE EDGE

The feathered edge of a sheet of paper. Handmade papers can have four deckles made by the flow of pulp against the edge of the paper mold. Machinemade papers may have "fake" deckles made by "cutting" the paper with jets of water or air.

FRISKET PAPER

A transparent waterproof tissue, with or without a light adhesive back. It is used to mask off areas when painting, retouching photos, making french mats or mat bevels.

GLASSINE

A glossy translucent paper used as an interleaving paper for photos, negatives, stamps and canvas.

HOT PRESS

A smooth finish on paper and boards. Also called High or Plate finish. Good surface for pen and ink work.

JAPANESE PAPER

Incorrectly called "Rice" paper. There are hundreds of varieties of this lightweight, soft, very strong paper. Used for watercolor, pen and ink and conservation work.

KRAFT PAPER

A strong coarse paper made from wood pulp. Most often available in white, black and brown. Used for wrapping and dust covers. Black kraft is sometimes used to make brass rubbings.

PAPYRUS

A writing material invented by the Egyptians. Made from the stalks of the papyrus plant. The stalks are cut into thin slices and woven into a flat sheet. The sheet is then beaten or put under pressure to bind the woven pieces.

PARCHMENT

Genuine parchment is made from animal skins. It has been used for important documents such as wills, deeds and diplomas. Because of its high cost, it is not used as often as it used to be.

PARCHMENT PAPER

Also called vegetable parchment. It is made by dipping an unsized paper into a special acid bath then washing and drying it under pressure. This makes the paper very strong and partly transparent. Art parchment is made from ordinary wood pulp but has the appearance and surface of vegetable parchment. Used for documents, certificates and calligraphy work.

PRINTMAKING PAPERS

Used for lithography, etchings, serigraphs and other printing processes. Papers are often 100% rag and have a soft thick feel. They can also have a hot press finish.

NEWSPRINT

Made of groundwood pulp. This is the same paper that newspapers are printed on. A very poor quality paper - strickly used for temporary work. Exposed to light and heat it will turn brown and brittle very quickly.

WATERCOLOR PAPER

The best watercolor papers are hand or mold made of 100% rag. They have been hard sized to accept watercolors so the paint will not run and yet not soak in too deeply. The most popular size is 22 x 30. It is available in several weights including 72lb., 140lb., and 300lb. These numbers refer to the weight of a ream (500 sheets) of paper 22 x 30. The 300lb. is almost a thick board and has very little buckling or warping. An artist using lighter weights should soak and stretch their paper so that it will not buckle when in use. You can flatten watercolor paper in the heat press but it is only a temporary pressing — as soon as humidity sets in it will return to its buckled state. Dry mounting is possible and permanent but not recommended for valuable works of art.

5

Matting

Matting is the border that surrounds the art within a picture frame. Several materials could be used as a mat. However, most often it is made of mat board. Mat board is made of several layers that include the lining paper on the backside, the center core and the cover sheet. The cover sheet carries the color. There are many manufacturers that make this special board for the framing industry. Mat board is available in hundreds of colors and finishes. The standard size is 32" x 40".Several other sizes have become available due to the popularity of oversize graphics. Board quality will depend on the materials and methods used by the manufacturer.

Although mat boards have been specially treated by manufacturers to last for many years — matting and framing is not forever. It is important for a customer to understand that the environment affects framing just as it affects anything else in their home. Therefore a valued piece should be brought in to the shop every three to five years for refreshing and cleaning. This practice would not only be of service to our customer it would bring more business to our shops.

Matting is an art. Like any art it requires knowledge of materials and methods and refinement of skills. Not only are proper cutting techniques required but the understanding of color and proportion of the mat in relationship to the art is very important. Matting provides two significant features to framed art — presentation and protection.

PRESENTATION

The purpose of picture framing is to present the item to be framed in the best possible manner. Matting can be used to enhance the piece being framed. A mat can highlight a color, accent a shape, and of course increase the size of the piece. Matting is used on flat art — art on paper, newsprint, certificates, photos, posters etc. Matting is not used on paintings. Paintings on canvas or similar material are not glassed, therefore a wood liner serves to present the piece. Matting is usually, but not always, covered by glazing.

Mat cutting and decoration is truly an art. Picture framers can develop their skills in cutting through practice. Mat board can be a creative material to cut by machine and by hand. Boards can be cut, layered, painted and covered to create a good presentation for any art piece being framed.

PROTECTION

The most important feature of matting is the protection it provides. The border and its immediate backing provide support for the artwork.

The artwork can be attached within the mat unit allowing it to expand and contract with the change of temperature. Methods used to attach the art must not restrict the piece. For example, if you hold down a piece of art at all four corners, buckling will result because the piece had no expansion room. This restriction forced the piece to buckle in the center area. All paper items need to be supported. Matting provides

support and permits air circulation which allows any moisture that may condense within the frame to dissipate.

An alternative to matting would be mounting. This is a complete, permanent restriction of the piece — not a conservation method — just a presentation method. Any restriction of a piece must be full, that is a solid, complete mount such as dry or wet mounting, rather than the occasional tape or glue.

Matting methods and materials should be used with regard to the value of the piece to the customer. Any item to be framed SHOULD NOT be put directly against the glass. The result will be buckling, wrinkles, mold formation, and items "sticking" to the glass. Realizing that there are many customers that will insist that a piece be put into a frame without a mat and up against the glass — you must be prepared to explain the pros and cons of such a practice. If the piece is mounted a spacer should be used to keep it away from the glass.

Using the classic "decorator" style of putting a picture between two pieces of glass will also cause wrinkles. You can use a spacer between the glasses to allow the piece to move with the temperature change or fully mount the piece. Wrinkles and buckles are not good for the art piece but even worse are the problems it causes with angry customers and a workroom filled with pieces to be re-done.

Any time a "no mat" situation exists remember the piece needs room to breathe and support. If, despite all this advice, you insist on putting the paper art into a frame without any support and smack up against the glass — what will happen? The following illustrations show the types of wrinkles and buckling that will result.

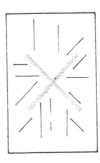

PROPORTION

Proportion is something one sees rather than measures. It is a visual balance of light, color, texture, shapes, and line direction. When everything is the right size, is in the right place, and has the right intensity, you have achieved good composition and balance of proportion. When you design framing for your customers, you should seek such a balance of all the elements — the artwork, the matting, and the frame. Perhaps you have a background in art and have developed "an eye" for proportion. If not, practice will help you to develop one.

Every product has been designed. Some designs, of course, are better than others. Each building, postcard, teakettle, pin, table, etc. had to be designed. So it is with framing. Your job as a framer is to present every piece well. The requests of your customers will place some restrictions on you, but always try to make the artwork "comfortable" in the frame — in harmony with the other elements.

The relationship between the artwork and where it will hang is also important. Ask your customer about the intended location. If the customer plans to hang a simple primitive painting on busy wallpaper, you will need to select framing that will give the artwork "room to breathe."

No matter what you are framing — a shoe, an original pen and ink, a coin, a certificate — each piece has a design that should be enhanced by the framing. The following descriptive words may describe the piece; they will also help determine the type of framing that will be suitable for it.

Coloring: light, dark, intense, dull
Lines: delicate, broad, busy, strong
Shapes: small, large, mixed, solid
Texture: delicate washes, thick paint

On this page are examples of matting for an 8" x 10" picture. Some are just okay, while others are more "in proportion." The following page gives more examples. Look them over and compare. Which ones do you prefer?

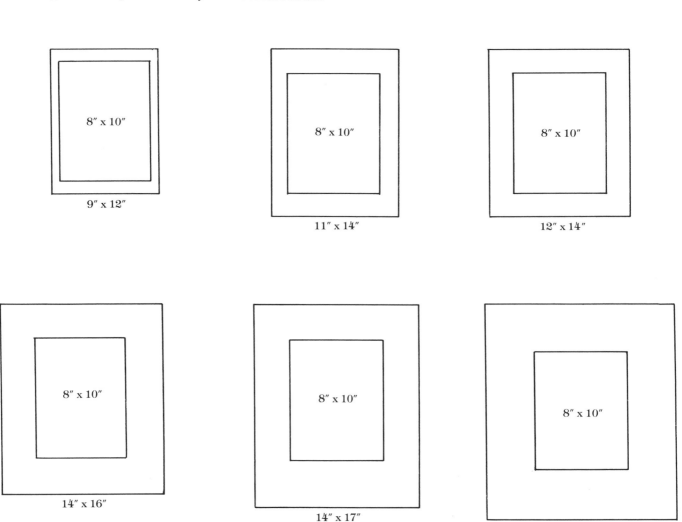

8" x 10"
9" x 12"

8" x 10"
11" x 14"

8" x 10"
12" x 14"

8" x 10"
14" x 16"

8" x 10"
14" x 17"

8" x 10"
16" x 18"

Don't be afraid of large mat borders. They can create a visually pleasing "breathing space" between the artwork and the frame. Small, narrow mats tend to distract the eye with patterns of lines going around the artwork.

Should you "weight" the bottom of a mat? For some pieces it is the right thing to do, for others it is not. Cutting a mat with extra on the bottom was tradi-tional in the past. However, since the invention of the straightline mat cutter, it has been easier to cut the borders even on all sides. Which looks better? Which is more appropriate? There is no rule for this. It is a choice based on one's personal sense of proportion. It is through experience that you'll learn how to make these choices. Expand your thinking, experiment, feel free to try new designs.

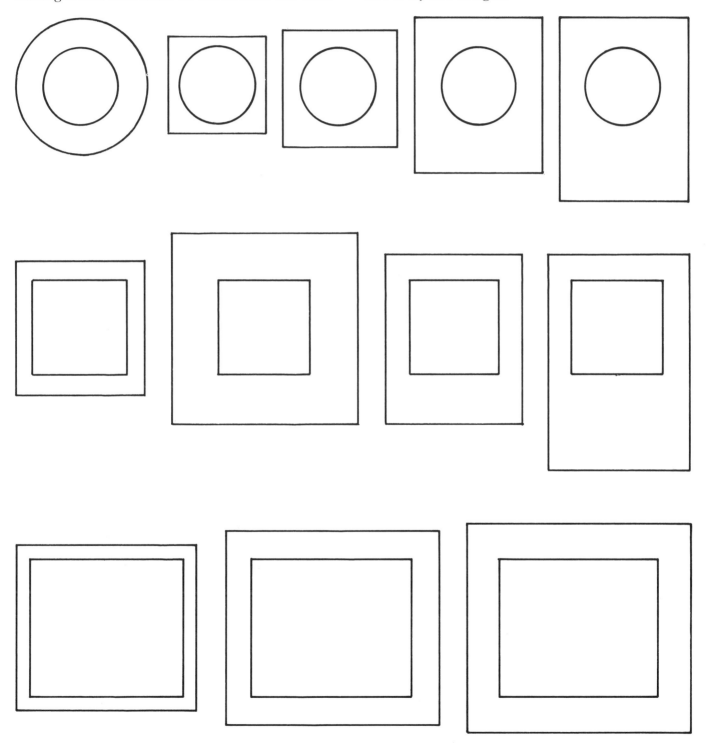

COLOR

As picture framers we should encourage our customers to choose the best environment for the piece they bring to us. If they like it enough to bring it into the shop — they want the best presentation for it. Color has everything to do with the well designed presentation. Choosing the right color does take practice. You have to know your mat boards — really know. Take out a print and put the corners on it and compare the colors. Note the subtle differences such as: French Gray is yellowish gray, Antique Buff has a very warm pinkish tone, and Mist has a very cool tone. There are several whites to choose from and you must learn the difference. Which whites are warm? cool? Just any white will not do for your customer's best presentation. There is a mat specifier in the back of this book, on the last page. There are seven different whites. If you spend enough time working with the corners on different prints you'll see the difference.

The best presentation you can give your customer is one where the piece is comfortable in its environment. The picture should harmonize with the framing presentation. How much color should you use? Let's try this creative exercise: picture this, if you will (as we say in the trade), a big expansive landscape, out in the farmlands of Ohio. In the lower lefthand corner, a thin wire fence winds up a slight hill leading us to the red brick farmhouse with gray shutters, a gray silo and white barn with a black roof — oops, forgot to mention — it's snowing like crazy! There's white stuff everywhere. What colors would this picture be most comfortable in? Our choices from the picture are white, brick red, gray and maybe we could really stretch to see the dried corn stalks so we could use tan. Look at the amounts of each color that are represented in the picture. The largest portion of color is white, with accents of gray, brick red, black and tan (corn stalks).

This picture would be most comfortable in white. The other colors could be used in the frame or liners. If you choose the brick red as the mat, it would look good but very "decorator." Taking a small amount of color and using it for the main mat will give a dramatic effect but is generally not the best presentation of the art. Taking into consideration that your customer may be more concerned with matching her couch than presenting the art — you'll probably use brick red.

Along with studying your mat colors, pay attention to the decorating trends. Colors are very trendy and often "date" pieces. Remember pink-beige in the 50s? Avocado green in the 60s? Blue and green, pink and red and orange and yellow in the 70s? And of course, a round of applause for gray and mauve in the 80s!

Study your mat colors. They can dramatically change the presentation you design.

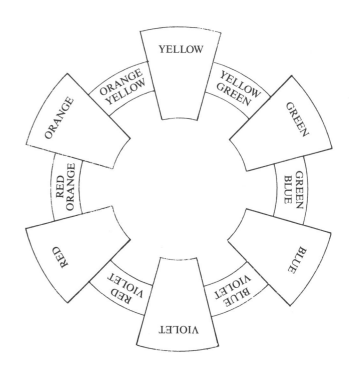

THE KEY WORDS OF COLOR

Hue is the name of a color. Red, yellow, blue, green, etc.

Shade is the color you get by adding black to a hue.

Tint is the color you get by adding white to a hue.

Value is the lightness or darkness of a color from black to white. Light values increase the size of any object. And dark values decrease the size of an object.

Intensity/Chroma is the brightness (full intensity) or dullness (low intensity) of a hue.

- Primary colors: red, yellow, blue
- Analogous is a color scheme using similar hues.
- Monochromatic is a color scheme using the variety of tints and shades from one particular hue.
- Neutrals — black, white, and grays.
- Complementary colors are the colors that are opposite one another on the color wheel.

MAT MATHEMATICS

To figure the dimensions of a mat, first determine the size of the opening (window) by measuring the artwork to be matted. The mat must overlap **each edge** of the artwork by **at least** 1/8″, in order to prevent those edges from peeking through (or actually popping through) the mat opening. For example, the usual opening for an 8″ x 10″ photo is 7-3/4″ x 9-3/4″. While measuring, remember that mats not only enhance artwork, they can also be used to cover spots, rips, or undesirable portions of the art. This is called "cropping," and it is a very convenient method for hiding defects without actually trimming the artwork. When measuring artwork to accommodate a signature or other significant markings, allow at least 1/4″ on all sides of the image or plate mark, with extra space allowed at the bottom — or — allow an equal amount of space on each side, determined by the amount required for the signature.

After the proper opening is established, add the amount of matting desired. Remember to add the amount of both side borders to the horizontal opening measurement, and both the top and bottom borders to the vertical opening measurement.

Example: 9″ x 12″ — this represents opening
    + 4″   4″ — this represents a 2″
_____ border each side
   13″ x 16″ — this is your **outside** mat
          size

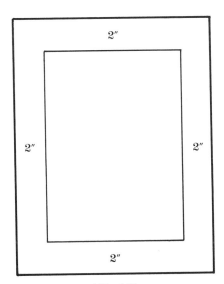

13″ x 16″

If you already have a frame to work with, then begin with the frame size, and subtract the desired mat opening to determine border size.

Example: 12″ x 16″ — this is the frame size
    - 8″ x 12″ — this is the opening size
_____
    4″   4″ — this represents a 2″
          border each side

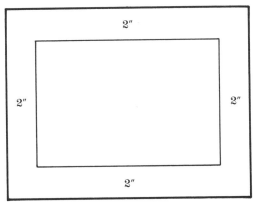

12″ x 16″

When matting will not be equal on all sides, either because chosen artwork does not fit chosen frame evenly, or because you prefer different proportions for the mat, it often looks best to divide the available border equally, or use extra at the bottom.

Example:
```
    11" x 14"  — this is the frame size
  -  8" x 10"  — this is the opening
    3"    4"   — make mat border either
                 1½" sides, 2" top and
                 bottom — or — 1½" top
                 and sides, 2½" bottom
```

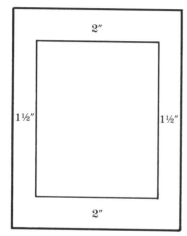

11" x 14"

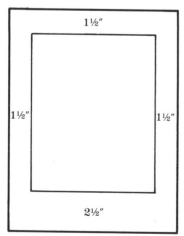

11" x 14"

Of course, many mat sizes will not allow you the convenience of working with whole inches. You will need to become familiar with adding, subtracting, and dividing fractions. For example:

A customer brings in an old frame which measures 14-1/2" x 21-3/4". No matter how you fudge it, the best mat opening for the vertical picture the customer wants in the frame is 8-3/4" x 15".

So:
```
    14-1/2" x 21-3/4"  — frame size
  -  8-3/4" x 15"      — mat opening
    5-3/4"    6-3/4"   — available border
```

After discussing the possible ways of using the unequal matting with the customer, it is decided that the mat border will be the same on top and at sides, with extra at the bottom. Divide the 5-3/4" in half to determine the side border. It will be 2-7/8" each side. Since this will also be the top border amount, subtract 2-7/8" from the 6-3/4" you have available. This leaves 3-7/8", which will be the lower mat border.

Don't be intimidated by fraction work — it just takes a little practice.

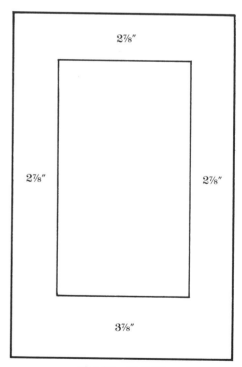

14-1/2" x 21-3/4"

DOUBLE MATS

Double mats allow a narrow strip of matting (called a "lip") to accent the inner edge of the main mat. There are two approaches to cutting double mats.

METHOD A:

Cut your bottom mat, the one that will rest directly on the artwork, first. This bottom mat is also called the "undermat" or "liner mat." Measure and cut this as you would any single mat. To figure the window size of the top mat, which will be cut separately, use the opening and border size of the liner as your guide. Decide how much of the undermat is going to show —frequently 1/4" each side, but it may be 1/8", 1/2", or some other amount each side. The top mat border will be **that much smaller** than the undermat border on **each side.** Then do your figuring.

Example: The opening for the artwork measures 8" x 10". You have decided on a 3" border each side.

So: 8" x 10" — opening for liner mat
     + 6"   6" — 3" border each side
     ──────────────
      14" x 16" — outside size for liner mat

You decide to allow a 1/4" lip to show on each side.

So: 8"   x 10"   — liner opening
     +   1/2"   1/2" — 1/4" lip showing
     ──────────────
      8-1/2" x 10-1/2" — opening for top mat

Now that you know the opening for the top mat, figure it in the usual way:

      14"   x 16"   — outside size
     - 8-1/2"   10-1/2" — opening for top mat
     ──────────────
      5-1/2" x 5-1/2" — 2-3/4" border each side

You may prefer to think of it this way: The undermat border is 3" each side, and you want 1/4" of this border to show all around; so subtract 1/4" from 3" = 2-3/4" border. You can simply begin with a board 14" x 16", and cut a 2-3/4" border each side.

Align the liner mat beneath the top mat, with the lip exposed evenly, and adhere together with double-sided tape or glue.

METHOD B:

In this method, the top mat is cut first. Follow mathematical procedures as in method A to determine top mat border, then cut it. Save the "fallout," the piece removed from the center of the mat. Now cut a board for the undermat — make it about 1/4" or so shorter than the outside width and length size of the top mat. Using the example from method A, this board would be about 13-3/4" x 15-3/4".

Place the top mat face down, and apply double-sided tape to all four sides. Adhere top mat to under-mat board (with front of undermat board against back of top mat). Apply a small strip of double-sided tape to the back of the fallout piece, and replace it in the mat opening, pressing to adhere it to the undermat board. Lay this double-board unit face down, and cut liner mat according to the border size determined. As mentioned before, this amount will be **more** than the top mat border, determined by the amount of lip you want to show.

Although smaller board pieces may be used for liner mats (since only a small amount will show), this practice is not recommended, because the "dropoff" where the undermat ends may cause buckling in the fit job.

The methods described for cutting double mats are also used to cut triple mats, etc.

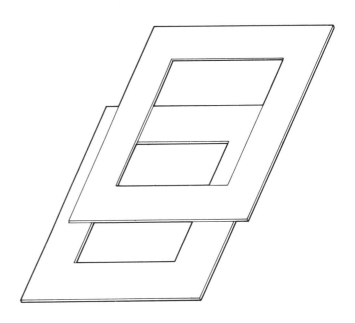

STANDARD SIZES

4 x 5	12 x 16	26 x 32
4 x 6	14 x 18	30 x 40
5 x 7	16 x 20	32 x 40
6 x 8	18 x 24	36 x 48
8 x 10	20 x 24	40 x 48
8½ x 11	22 x 28	40 x 60
9 x 12	24 x 30	48 x 96
11 x 14	24 x 36	

1/32" means the inch has been broken into 32 equal pieces and you are measuring 1 part of it — 1/32".

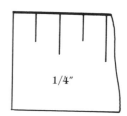

1/4 means 1 of 4 equal pieces.

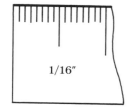

1/16 means 1 of 16 equal pieces.

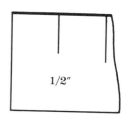

1/2 means 1 of 2 equal pieces.

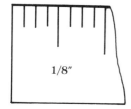

1/8 means 1 of 8 equal pieces.

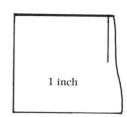

1 inch

The solid inch without any pieces.

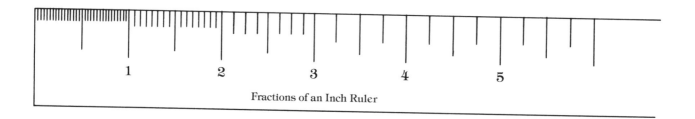

Fractions of an Inch Ruler

CUTTING UP A MAT BOARD

Mat boards are available in three sizes: 32″ x 40″, 40″ x 48″ and 40″ x 60″. The most common size is 32″ x 40″.

In the following illustrations, each 32″ x 40″ board has been cut entirely into pieces of the same standard size, as indicated. When ordering boards, it is important to consider how many mats and corresponding back boards can be cut from a sheet.

For practical purposes, you will seldom use a whole board economically, since you will rarely have a request for eight mats and backs of the same color. Framers have tried to make use of their scrap boards — but they still build up. After a while you'll just have to get rid of them.

These illustrations are to show you how much you waste when cutting up a board. If you cut a 20″ x 24″, you still have enough for another 20″ x 24″ (the backing), however, if you cut a 22″ x 28″ you'll not have enough for a backing and will have to cut another board. Don't forget to include that in your pricing.

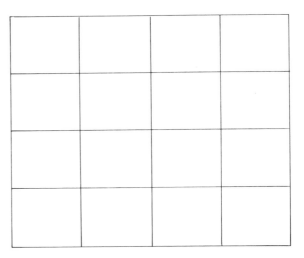

8″ x 10″

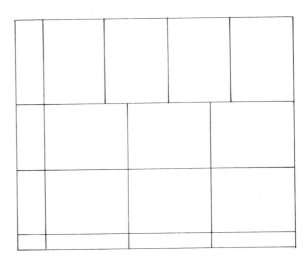

9″ x 12″

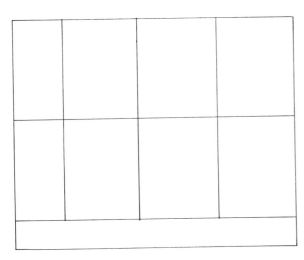

11″ x 14″

12″ x 16″

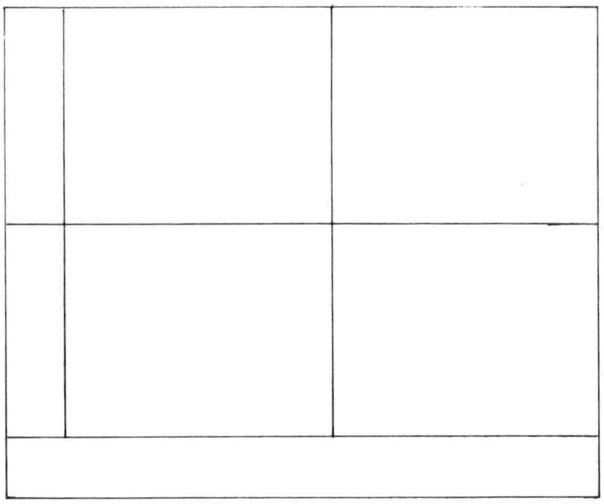

14″ x 18″

16″ x 20″

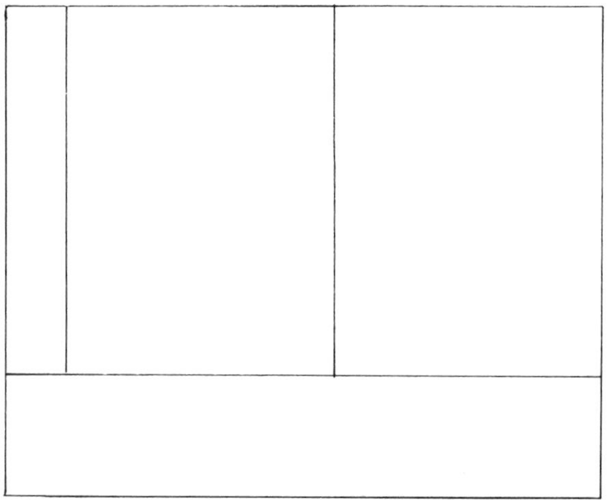

18″ x 24″

20″ x 24″

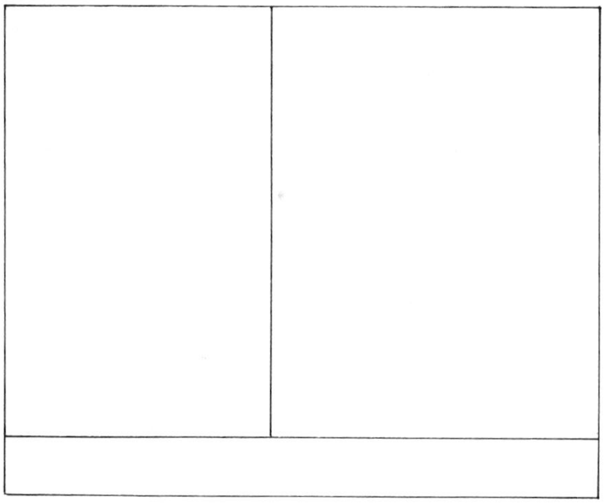

22″ x 28″

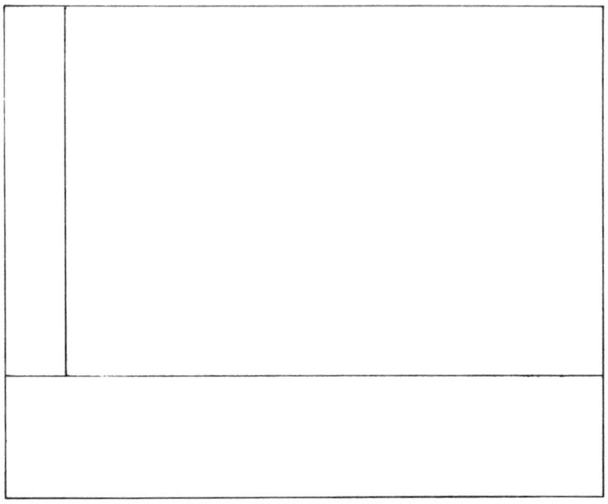

24″ x 36″

HOW TO CUT A MAT

TRIMMING THE MAT BOARD TO SIZE

Determine the outside size of the mat. Using a wall mounted cardboard and glass cutter open bottom clamp, slip the board onto the ledge, line it up with the measurements on the left hand side. Close the bottom clamp.

Engage the cutting head and pull downward until you reach the bottom. Open the clamp to release the board. Repeat the process on the remaining side. This machine should be kept square. Check it weekly and adjust it if necessary. If you start out with an unsquare mat board, your window mat will also be out of square.

You can use your straight line mat cutter to trim boards to size if you have a squaring arm attachment. The squaring arm attaches to the right hand side of the mat cutter base. On the right side of the cutting head is the straight cutting blade. Lift the handle of the mat cutter and insert the board to be trimmed. You may have to take off the mat guide on the left hand of the cutter, if it gets in the way. Set the mat board under the center bar and up against the squaring arm. Adjust the position of the board to cut to size. Set the handle of the mat cutter down to hold the board still. Engage the cutting head by pushing in a little pin on the right side of the head. This pin will keep the straight cutting head locked into position. To cut pull the head towards you until you reach the bottom. Keep this square by measuring it often and adjusting it.

Other methods of cutting the board to size are covered on page 41.

SLIP SHEETS

Several mat cutters have a space cut into the wood base. This cut out area is used to accommodate the depth of the blade as it extends through the mat board. It is possible to cut mats directly on the board using the cut out area. However, there is a better way. Using a slip sheet will give you cleaner cuts without any ragged edges. You will find it even more effective while cutting rag board.

Slip sheets are scraps of mat board (do not use thick mounting board) six inches wide by any convenient length that is longer than the mat to be cut. You will find that you will have many scraps left from your everyday work that will be useable as slip sheets. Your mat will be pressed tightly between the cutter bar and the slip sheet. This will cause the board to compress. When the blade enters the mat it will slice cleanly through the mat rather than "push" through, causing rough edges on the face of the mat.

Bottom clamp on wall mounted cutter.

Pull downward until blade passes through entire board.

Pin on right side of cutter head will lock head in cutting position.

55

HOW TO CUT A SINGLE-OPENING MAT

1) Cut a mat board to the outside measurements.
2) Adjust the mat guide for the correct size border.
3) Stand at the bottom of the cutter and lift the handle, place the mat board face down on the slip sheet.
4) Hold the mat board firmly against the edge of the mat guide.
5) Using a pencil, draw a line that will act as a guide for the cutter head — the intersecting lines will show you where to start and stop your cut.
6) Slide the cutting head up to the top of the mat.
7) Put your right hand on the cutter. The most comfortable position will be to rest the index and middle finger on the bevel cutter knob. Place your thumb loosely under the large knurled screw on the side of the head.
8) Push down with your two fingers on the blade — taking care to insert the blade smoothly, rather than jabbing it down into the board.
9) Insert the blade approx. 3/16″ above the intersecting lines. Continue to slide the cutting head down until you come to the lower intersection. Pass the intersection by 3/16″ then release the cutter head — it will pop up.
10) Lift the handle slightly with your left hand while you turn the mat board to the next side with your right hand — so that you may cut the second side as you did the first.
11) Continue around the four sides — taking care the cutout does not tear at the corners.
12) If you have "short cut" the mat, do not pull the cutout — the corner will tear. Instead, use a single edge razor blade. Slip the blade through the face of the mat, at the same angle as the cut, and finish the cut to the corner.

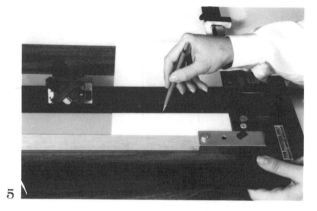

5

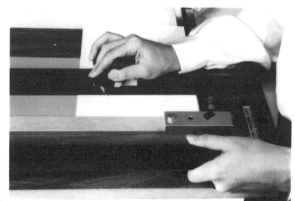

8

9

12

HOW TO CUT AN OVAL MAT

HOW TO CUT AN OVAL

Oval mats need to be cut with a machine that can correctly outline an ellipse. It is nearly impossible to cut one by hand.

The following directions are for oval cutter that "hangs" over the mat board rather than one that is nailed down or used free hand.

1) Position the trimmed mat board face up in the center of the cutter. There are special rules that can be attached, if they are not already a part of the machine, that are used to find the center.

2) If you have difficulty with shifting boards you can hold the board still with a couple of staples in the center, as pictured at the right.

3) To cut an oval opening 8″ x 10″, set the lower scale at 8″ and the upper one at 2″ — the difference between the width and length of the oval.

4) Bring the side hold bars over to rest on the edges of the mat board.

5) Bring the top handle down to lower the cutter onto the mat board.

6) Using two hands on the top knobs, start at 3 o'clock and moving clockwise around the oval, apply as even a pressure as possible. You do not have to cut all the way through the first time around - twice around should give you a nice clean cut.

7) Lift top handle upward to release the cut mat board.

8) There are several knives available that will give you different angle cuts and also an embosser that will give a nice neat accent to ovals and circles.

9) Depending on the specific oval cutter, there are several measuring devices and attachments available to make the positioning easier.

10) This same machine can be used to cut oval and circular glass too.

2

6

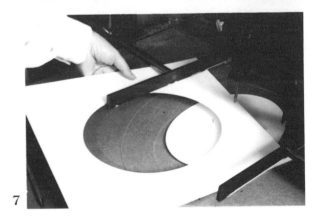

7

CONSERVATION

Picture framers are not conservators, however, we have a responsibility to our customers to preserve their work in the best possible environment. To maintain the condition of the piece, store it properly and encase it in a frame job that will not harm it.

More and more fine artwork is being done on paper — serigraph, collage, lithography, etchings, and even fine quality offset reproductions. Along with the typical artwork we must include family photos, personal documents and certificates. Many of them are valuable to the customer and irreplaceable.

Art on paper has many enemies — light, heat, humidity, air pollution and itself — sometimes art work is done on faulty paper with fugitive media and may deteriorate because of its inherent faults.

As art on paper becomes more popular, we are faced not only with framing it but also with preserving it. To understand what can be done, you have to understand what can go wrong.

First, we have to deal with the inherent faults of the work itself. The paper the artist has used as a base for the work may not be of the finest quality. Even the finest handmade papers may have serious defects from the various processes and chemicals used to make them. We must also consider the medium the artist has used to create the image — whether or not the inks, paints or drawing materials are permanent and colorfast or perhaps too strong for the paper that they have been applied to. Application of the medium could be by hand or by machinery at various speeds and the quality could vary greatly. Obviously, the artist should have control over the paper, the medium and the application. The artist's signature shows approval of all three elements.

In order to protect the paper and the image, we must first consider the environment.

Light is hard for us to control because of its everyday presence and because we need it to view and enjoy our collections. All light fades works of art on paper. Even the smallest amount of light affects the condition of the work. Printers and artists may use the finest paints, inks and chalks; however, they will all deteriorate with exposure. It would be wise to guard against unnecessary exposure. Pictures should never be hung in direct sunlight; even reflected, indirect daylight is a source of highly destructive ultraviolet light.

Ultraviolet rays accelerate fading of the media and even deteriorate the paper itself. Fluorescent lights are a very strong source of ultraviolet light. They can be covered with special plastic sleeves to filter out the dangerous radiation. An acrylic sheeting is available which may be used in framing to filter these ultraviolet rays. The sheeting is available in grades from 0

to 5, with 5 being the strongest. Unfortunately, it also has an amber tone to it which alters the appearance of the work.

Heat accelerates the deterioration of paper. You should warn your customers of the dangers of hanging valuable pictures over the fireplace. High temperatures also generate soot that will penetrate the piece. Valuable pictures should not hang over radiators or heat registers either.

Excessive humidity brings the threat of mold. Humidity exceeding 70 percent will encourage the growth of mold. A humidity level of 50 percent is ideal. When hanging or storing pictures, beware of dampness on outside walls or in basements and cellars. Mold growth in paper often appears as rusty patches that discolor the sheet.

It is very important that the artwork **not touch the glass**. Condensation of moisture will encourage mold growth which in turn will destroy the picture. Circulation of air is important as it reduces the chances of mold growth.

Some insects find paper art and/or the media very tasty. Silverfish, termites, cockroaches and woodworms prefer warm, damp and dark places to live. They are a serious threat to works of art on paper and to books. They will eat their way through pictures to get to the glue sizing or starch paste that may be used in the framing process. Although termites and woodworms prefer wood, they will eat anything made of cellulose, including paper. Cockroaches come out at night and prefer parchment, leather, paper, fabrics and any adhesives or media with sugar.

Thanks to modern living we have a multitude of **gases** in the air. Sulphur dioxide, which is produced from fossil fuels like coal and oil, is the major contributor. Sulphur dioxide attacks paper and causes discoloration and embrittlement and, eventually, the disintegration of the paper fibers. Certain artists' pigments, because of their chemical content, will react with the sulphur dioxide and cause destruction of the paper or discoloration of the pigments.

We cannot escape air pollution. Air conditioning will help control the pollution and the heat and humidity. Paper manufacturers are producing papers and boards with buffers which aid in neutralizing the damaging effects of pollution.

Artwork done on paper, such as etchings, lithography, silkscreen, collage, watercolors and offset reproductions, require matting. Matting is the border around a picture placed between the picture and the frame. Matting is both aesthetic and utilitarian. It serves to create a pleasing balance around the artwork and protects the artwork in both handling and framing.

Artwork should never be placed directly against the glass. Glass easily condenses moisture, which will encourage the growth of mold and increase the risk of the artwork sticking to the glass. The mat creates a breathing space and allows the picture to move in response to changing atmospheric conditions. You may have noticed during times of high humidity that paper art buckles. This is natural. During dry temperatures it will contract and appear to be almost flat.

There are several types of matting boards available for use in conservation framing. All products — boards, tapes, and adhesives — should be acid-free, non-deteriorating products.

Standard mat board is made with a wood pulp center core, which is similar to common newspaper and like newspaper, ages quickly. The aging process is accelerated because of the high acidic content of the pulp. The chemicals not only destroy the mat board itself, but they also destroy the artwork they touch or come close to.

Recently a company introduced a standard mat board that is acid-free. The board has been treated with buffering agents to retard the aging and deterioration of the board.

Several manufacturers are constantly upgrading their products. Watch for new developments.

Past practices allowed standard mat board (without buffering) to be used in conjunction with museum boards. However, we now know the decay comes from the bevel of the mat. As the pulpboard self-destructs, the chemical reaction seeps out from the bevel onto the artwork. This is called acid burn. You have probably seen an acid burn on an older piece of artwork. It appears as a brown line close to the bevel and an all-over tan coloring on the face of the work. So you ask, "How long does it take for these mats to destroy artwork?" It depends — anywhere from a couple of months to a couple of years. The environment would accelerate the corrosive action.

The safest matting board to use for fine artwork is rag board, sometimes referred to as museum board. Rag board was developed in the 1940s at the request of our nation's museums to preserve their collections. It was not made of rags, however, but from scraps of pure cotton and linen and was most often off-white or cream. When looking at a profile of this board you do not see the plys or layers of paper that comprise the standard mat board. It is a solid sheet made of cotton fibers and available in several thicknesses. Rag board is now available with acid-free color sheets that are adhered to the face.

The basic window mat consists of the face sheet with a window cut to expose the artwork and to accommodate a signature or other significant markings. A space of at least a ¼″ should be allowed on all sides of the image or plate mark. The backing board

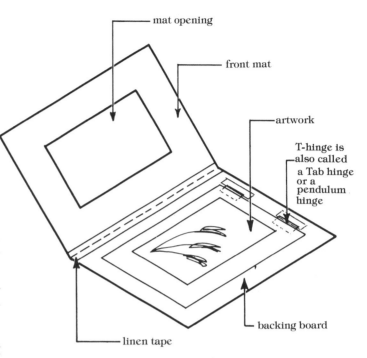

mat opening

front mat

artwork

T-hinge is also called a Tab hinge or a pendulum hinge

backing board

linen tape

The proper presentation of a fine work of art.

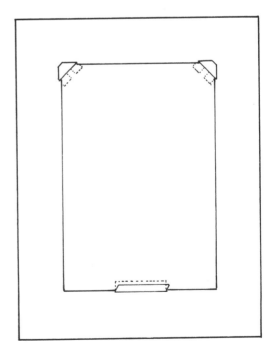

Corner pocket/trough made of Mylar or Barrier paper. Attached with ATG tape.

should also be made of rag. The artwork would be attached to the front of the backing boards, not to the window mat, and should be attached with proper hinging methods. The two boards are then attached to one another at the side or at the top. When this unit is placed in a frame, the filler board that is used must also be non-acidic. The use of standard mat boards would create an acidic environment, and should not be used at all. The acid from these boards would migrate to the artwork.

Should you have a contemporary picture that you feel would not be enhanced by a mat, the piece can be "floated" on a rag board with the use of Japanese paper hinges and kept away from the glass through the use of narrow spacers hidden under the rabbet of the frame.

A word about hinges: the method used to attach the artwork to the matting is very important. The hinge and its adhesive must be acid-free, water-reversible, non-staining, and strong enough to hold the artwork securely in place.

There are many types of Japanese papers available for use as hinging papers. For many years these papers have been called "rice papers" but this is a misnomer. They are not made of rice, but of cellulose fibers from a variety of bushes and trees available in Japan. Generally handmade, these papers have great strength because of their cellulose origin and method of manufacture. Japanese papers range in weight from a very thin silk tissue to a thick, rough sheet. Choose a paper that is lighter in weight than that of the artwork to be hinged: the hinge should be strong enough to take the shock of rough handling of the frame, but should give way if the artwork is put under great strain. Hinges may be torn from the paper rather than cut — a feathered edge will not show through the artwork or create an abrupt line.

The adhesive used in conjunction with the hinge must also comply with conservation standards. Although conservators disagree about which is the strongest, they do agree that the following are acceptable adhesives: wheat or rice starch, the traditional choice, which must be cooked in very small batches; and methyl cellulose paste, a more recent development which does not have to be cooked, just mixed with cold water.

Linen tape may also be used. The finest quality is made of white linen fabric coated with a wettable adhesive. This type of hinge and adhesive is used by libraries and museums as well as picture framers. The objection to this adhesive raised by some conservators is that its thickness and strength are too much for fine artwork. New developments in this area are expected very soon.

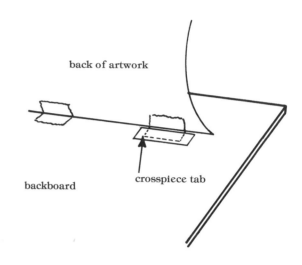

back of artwork

backboard

crosspiece tab

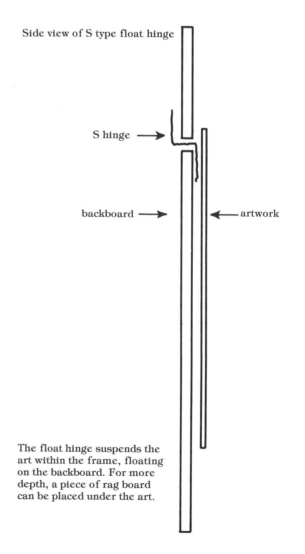

Side view of S type float hinge

S hinge

backboard

artwork

The float hinge suspends the art within the frame, floating on the backboard. For more depth, a piece of rag board can be placed under the art.

6

Mounting

MOUNTING

Mounting is a way to adhere a variety of papers and fabrics to different types of boards. There are several methods of mounting. This chapter will cover dry, wet, spray and PMA.

Different types of mounting will be suitable for different types of artwork. All mounting uses an adhesive and some form of pressure to bond the artwork to the board (substrate).

In all cases discussed, mounting requires the full adhesion of the article to the board.

Conservation procedures would not permit the full mounting as we will discuss here. Conservators would like any piece that is valued to be put into a frame with the least amount of restriction. Full mounting totally restricts the art. Needless to say mounting of framed items is very popular and very helpful to framers that want to restrict the movement of large flimsy items.

When choosing a mounting technique consider the suitability, adhesive, equipment, and risks. Mounting requires knowledge of the materials and plenty of practice. Before working on your customer's goods, gather several types of items and practice.

DRY MOUNTING

Dry mounting, also called heat mounting is a very reliable method. Items properly dry mounted will stay flat and bubble free. You will need a dry mount press and a heat activated adhesive. Dry mounting is fast, neat, and safe.

Successful dry mounting requires the monitoring of four variables: the amount of heat, time, pressure, and humidity. Humidity? Yes, HUMIDITY. Since varying amounts of moisture may be in the environment, it may become trapped between layers of papers and boards. The moisture can cause blisters and bubbles to form on the finished work.

PRESSURE is provided by the press. Pressure helps squeeze out the air from between the artwork, the adhesive tissue and the mounting board. This insures a good, tight contact among the three items.

HEAT is the temperature that is used to activate the adhesive tissue. There are many types of tissues, each with a specific activating temperature. Use the temperature suggested by the manufacturer of the adhesive. A slightly lower temperature is safer than a higher one.

TIME. The time period required to get a good bond varies most. Because of the different thicknesses and/or heat conducting characteristics of the item and the mounting board, the amount of time the unit is left in the press (dwell time) will vary. The recommended time on the tissue is a good place to start. In any case we are only talking seconds — not minutes. Because of the delicate surface or sensitivity to heat, an artwork to be mounted may take 10 to 20 seconds.

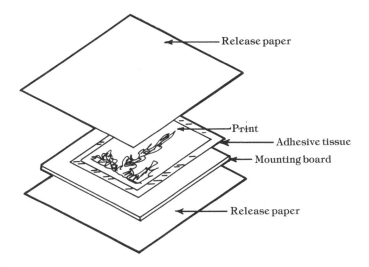

Release paper

Print

Adhesive tissue

Mounting board

Release paper

Each time you close the press to dry mount, you want to heat the adhesive tissue to its bonding temperature and hold that temperature for at least 10 to 15 seconds.

Companies that sell dry mounting tissue usually offer a sample packet containing all their tissues. Each tissue will be accompanied with a spec sheet to explain the requirements for use. Read — try out the tissues. There are probably more tissues than you have need for. Some tissues are permanent (great for posters) some are removable, and some have very low heat settings.

Any work done in a dry mount press is not limited in size. The press can handle a size that is twice the depth of its plate by any length you can handle.

THE PROCESS

Assemble the art, tissue, mounting board, and 2 sheets of release paper to protect the press from excess adhesive.

Set the press at the required temperature and allow it to warm up in the closed position.

Pre-dry the art and mounting board by placing each in the press for 15 to 30 seconds. The length of time depends on the thickness of the items and the humidity level.

Position the print and the adhesive on the mounting board. Trim off excess adhesive — it may fold over. Using the tacking iron, tack the print and the adhesive to the backing board in one corner. DO NOT tack directly on the face. Do not tack the entire edge of the print. Do not make an x in the center of the print. Do not tack all four corners or opposite corners. All you want to do here is hold the pieces together so you can slip them into the press without them moving about.

Put the mounting board with the tissue and the art into the press. Make sure you use a release paper to keep the press clean.

Watch the clock.

Take the unit out of the press. For best results especially with stubborn or resistant papers, cooling under a weight upon immediate removal from the press assures a complete bond. The weight can be metal plates or a large piece of 1/2″ plate glass.

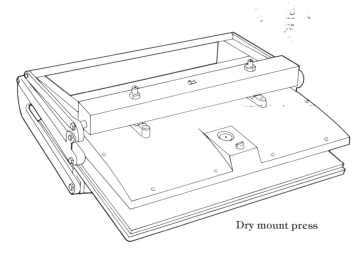

Dry mount press

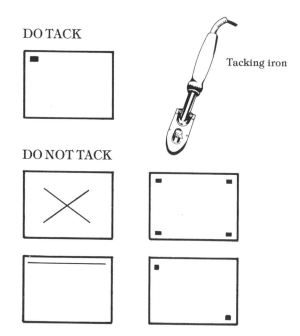

DO TACK

DO NOT TACK

Tacking iron

WET MOUNTING

Wet mounting is the oldest method of permanently adhering paper or fabric to a substrate (backing board). It does not require a press, however, wet mounting in combination with a vacuum press is very fast and effective.

The process requires you to use a wet paste in much the same fashion as you would when wallpapering. In our case we apply the paste to the substrate, dampen the print, put the two together, apply pressure and wait for the piece to dry.

There are adhesives in our industry especially made for this type of mounting. They usually state on the package if they are water-soluble and non-staining. They are available from general supply distributors and press manufacturers.

Supplies:
- a small soft roller — 2″ or wide stiff brush
- paste
- scrap of glass

1) Put the paste on the scrap of glass. That way the roller picks up an even amount.
2) Using a slightly damp clean sponge dab or lightly wipe the back of the print to be mounted. This expands the paper.
3) Apply paste to the backing board — very thin and as evenly as you can.
4) Cover face of print with clean paper. Set the print on the wet pasted backboard keeping the face cover in place. Start to smooth out the print starting from the middle outward using your hand or a soft rubber brayer. Keep the face cover on to protect the print from scratching.
5) Let dry under pressure for 6 - 8 hours. A piece of glass or metal plates will do. This is where a vacuum press would come in handy. With a vacuum press you not only get the pressure of the press you also have the moisture pulled out right away.

If a mistake has been made, dampen slightly with a sponge and lift gently, then re-apply. Remember wet paper tears easily.

Paste may be applied to the back of the print if it has no creases or wrinkles.

Canvas and other fabrics: Apply paste to the part that will receive the cloth. Allow paste to become tacky by exposure to the air. Carefully apply the fabric to the tacky surface. Keep the weave in the fabric in line with the backboard. Remember, the thinner the material, the thinner the application of glue and the faster everything dries.

VACUUM MOUNTING

The vacuum press applies pressure to make a bond by "drawing out" all the air in the press which forces the top and bottom of the press to come together as tight as possible. You can use spray adhesives or wet mounting pastes. The process of using the vacuum press with wet glues is very similar to the regular wet mounting process except instead of waiting for the paste to dry — the vacuum press will pull out all the moisture, which creates the bond immediately.

Any work done in the vacuum press is limited to the size of the press.

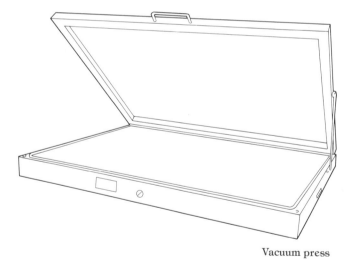

Vacuum press

SPRAYS

There are several spray adhesives available. A bond is achieved by applying pressure with a roller or a vacuum press. The vacuum press gives the best bond, with spray adhesives. Some very slick papers will resist the spray adhesives, especially during high humidity. Creating a very permanent bond with any spray is more difficult than with dry mounting.

Don't forget to control the spray. Wear a mask and use a ventilating fan to draw out the fumes.

PMA

Positional Mounting Adhesive is a sheet of adhesive made by 3M that is like a giant piece of double sided tape. It requires pressure to force the bond between the print and the mounting board. It will not stain, discolor or dry out. It is used primarily for smaller sized pieces no larger than 16x20.

Assemble the print, a mounting board and a piece of PMA. Peel off one side of the adhesive sheet and apply to the mounting board. Position the print over the mounting board and start to pull off the adhesive uncovering a little at a time. Set the print on the exposed area, careful not to get wrinkles or creases. Use a squeegee or roller type press to bond the three items together. This is also called "cold mounting".

REVERSING ADHESIVES

There are several solvents available that will remove or dissolve old adhesives and even recently applied permanent ones. Water will dissolve or remove wheat or rice starch, some linen tapes, and methyl cellulose paste. However, when it comes to removing permanent dry mount tissue or double-sided tape, you will need something stronger. Remember, that any solvent that is strong enough to dissolve a permanent adhesive is also very dangerous. Store all solvents along with other chemicals in a metal cabinet, away from heat. The solvents used by many framers are: Adhesive Release, Bestine thinner, mineral spirits, acetone, and carbon tetrachloride. All have their own properties allowing removal of different substances. Try them in an obscure corner to test their suitability. These solvents are to be used in well ventilated areas. Open doors, and turn on fans, if you do not have a spray booth to pull out the fumes. Put the solvent in containers such as Valvespout, available in an art supply store. This will control the flow of the liquid.

7

Fitting

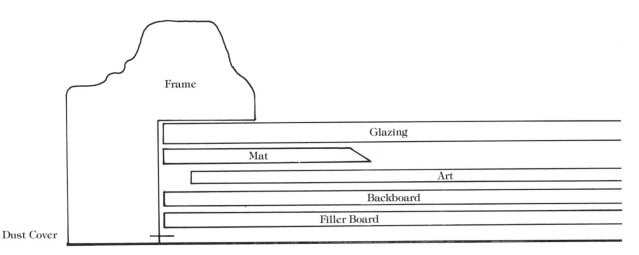

Cutaway of a Typical Frame Job

THE SANDWICH FIT

This fitting process has been in use at Kistler Art and Framing since 1971. It is called a sandwich fit because of the way the glass, mat, art and backboard is assembled. This is a "one time fit" — you won't have to open a job again to chase a piece of dust. This fit also serves as a moisture barrier for frame jobs that will hang in a bathroom.

- Clean glass.
- Brush off matted art and backboard.
- Set clean glass on the face of the matted art and backboard
- Run a strip of 3/4″ tape across the face of the glass, allowing only 1/8″ to sit on the face of the glass. Snap off the tape when you reach the edge.
- Wrap the remaining 5/8″ of the tape around to form a "U" channel to hold together the 3 items.
- Finish the remaining three sides in the same manner.

Applying 810 tape to edge of glass.

- Place the frame face down on a clean work table.
- Place the taped unit into the frame, add a filler board.

- Using a brad driver or point driver secure the pieces into the frame. Do not apply too much pressure. If you force the fit eventually it will create buckles in the art and mat.

- Apply glue or double sided tape to the back edge of the frame. If you are using glue, be careful not to leave any on the finish of the frame — it discolors the finish over a period of time.
- Place the dust cover paper on the adhesive — pull it taut.

- Using a trimming knife or razor blade, trim the paper at the edge of the frame. A slight angle to the blade will give a nice clean edge.

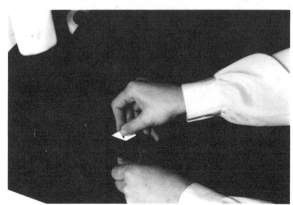

- Use an awl to poke a hole in the wood before putting in the screw eye. Hardwood frames will require drilling of the hole — by hand drill or electric. Insert the screw eyes. Use "fat" screw eyes for soft woods and the thinner ones for hardwoods (pre-drill, of course).
- Slip the shaft of the awl into the eye and twist it around. If you force the eye into the wood too fast you may weaken the eye.

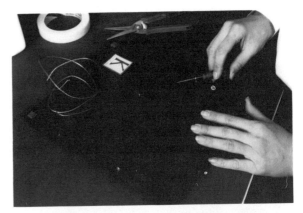

- Choose a wire that has a breaking strength of 3 times the weight of the picture. Insert the wire into the screw eye twice and pull tightly. Wrap the excess wire around very neatly — no wild crazy wrapping here. Wrap about 1″ and cut off the extra. Do not crimp — it may break some of the wires. Squeeze the loose wires into the wrap so it is neat.
- Put on your label and two bumper pads on the bottom two corners of the frame. The bumper pads help to hold the picture still while it is hanging and also aid air circulation which is important to the longevity of the picture.

FITTING PAINTINGS

There are several methods of holding a canvas painting in a frame. Valuable canvases should not have any attachments made directly to the wood bars. The offset clip would be the best suited to any valuable piece. They are available in many sizes. Seal off the back of a painting with a dust cover paper to keep out dirt and bugs. If more protection is needed a piece of cardboard, with holes punched in it for air circulation, should be attached.

STRETCHER BARS are available in lengths from 8″ to 60″ from art supply stores and distributors. They are made with a tongue and groove, mitered corners and beveled sides. They measure 1-3/4″ wide and about 7/8″ thick. Stock length can be purchased in regular and heavy duty width.

STRAINERS are solid, flat pieces of wood that can be either mitered or straight cut and assembled with glue and nails. They are generally used as support for weak frames or covered with a cardboard/fabric to support several types of art work.

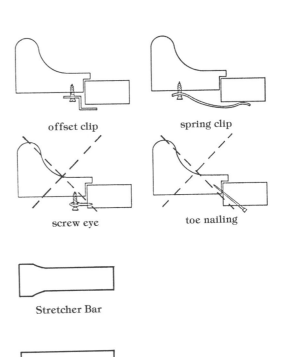

offset clip   spring clip

screw eye   toe nailing

Stretcher Bar

Strainer

MISCELLANEOUS FITTING SUPPLIES

The Expert Fitting Tool is used to insert brads into the back of the frame job. It works very smoothly. Very handy when fitting something you do not want to shake up, like pastels and shadow boxes.

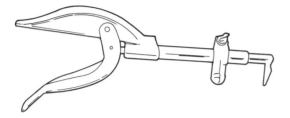

Wire is available in many strengths. Each number of wire has a breaking strength. Choose a strength that is about 3 times the weight of your picture, for example: the picture weighs 10 lbs. so you use 30 lb. strength which is number one wire. Stock about 3 to 4 numbers of wire to give you a selection.

Screw eyes are available in regular or long shank. Thick ones for softwood. Thin ones for hardwood. Drill before putting in the larger or longer ones. Excessive twisting will weaken or break the eye.

Screw Eyes

Linen hanger is for use on very lightweight paper items. Perhaps a small dry mounted print. They are applied by wetting the backside. Let the adhesive "set up", then apply.

Decorative hangers are available in many styles from the very plain to oriental motifs. If they have to be screwed in the top of the frame, the holding power would be limited. Also the customer will want a decorative nail to hang it on.

These heavy hangers are screwed into the backside of the frame. They can be used with or without wire. If the picture is very heavy, do not use wire. Line up the hooks in the wall with the hangers.

Traditional hanger used for hanging pictures. You can get these packaged to give to your customers as a goodwill gesture. It will give you a chance to explain how to hang it properly.

Turn buttons are used for removable backs on the backside of a frame job. They can be either screwed or nailed in.

8
Handling Artwork

All artwork put into a frame unit will have to be supported. If artwork is placed in the frame job and just packed in, with backing, it will buckle. Some people think that if it is packed very tightly it won't — but the reverse is true — the tighter the piece is put in the more it will ripple and buckle.

Attachment should be made at the top edge only, because the artwork must have room to expand and contract in response to changes in humidity. Do not attach artwork to its support on all four sides. Restriction of movement is one of the primary causes of buckling. The artwork must be either hung from the top edge or fully mounted.

There are several methods of attaching the artwork to its supporting boards.

Attaching artwork to the window mat is the easiest because you can tell when the artwork is centered properly in the opening. You can apply one or several pieces of tape to hold it in place — careful not to stretch the tapes — they will contract later on and wrinkle the picture.

Attaching it to the backing board takes a bit more time to center properly, however, it is a preferred method because it is more supportive. The backing board is stronger because it is solid. The window mat is weaker because the middle has been cut out. The artwork suspended from the top of the window mat will constantly "pull down" and eventually cause a gap between the mat and the artwork. This is especially noticeable on larger pieces.

Another way to attach artwork, with no visible means of support, is to "float" it. This method requires you to make a slice in the backing board and slip the tape through it. It will be easy to adjust the placement of the artwork floating on the backboard and very secure. The v-hinge is another way to float, however it is not as secure as the "S" style float hinge.

The choice of adhesive is an important consideration. If the artwork is valuable, or may be in the future, you must use acid-free, water-reversible adhesives, which can be completely removed without affecting the artwork. These include methyl cellulose and cooked wheat or rice starch. These adhesives are applied to torn strips of Japanese paper to make narrow pieces to serve as hinges. Linen tape is another acid-free tape, however, the drawback is that it's thick. Often too thick for the piece being framed, thereby causing ridges in the artwork. However, it is a good tape for heavy work such as watercolors done on 300 lb. paper and paper castings.

Polyvinyl tapes such as 3M's 810 tape are suitable adhesives for the majority of practical framing jobs, in which the artwork to be framed is of minimal value. These tapes are strong, stable, and clean but are not truly reversible. Do not use cellophane, surgical, filament, or masking tapes or rubber cement. These gum based adhesives dry out and leave deep stains on the paper.

Attaching art to the backing board by applying tape to the top front side.

Attaching art to the window mat by applying tape across the top backside.

Side view of a float hinge. The hinge strips are pulled through the backing board then secured.

Using double sided tape to hold the art down is okay to use on sturdy prints. However, you will find it too strong for the thinner papers. It will not let the thinner papers expand, causing wrinkles around the taped area.

SUGGESTED METHODS FOR HANDLING ART

The following methods are several ways to handle the many different items your customers may bring in to you. This concise list does not deal with the value of the items, only methods of handling them. Remember to consider how valuable an item may be before handling it. Conservation methods may differ from "practical" methods.

ART ON PAPER

- Examples: reproductions, limited editions, woodcuts, posters, engravings, etchings, lithographs, silkscreens, pen & ink, pastel, charcoal, etc.
- General rule: If you can roll it, it must be matted to support it within the frame.
- ALL paper art SHOULD be matted and glassed. Stress the use of museum matting if the art is worthy — having either sentimental or monetary value.
- Mat opening usually starts 1/4" away from the edge of the art or plate mark — more space may be allotted to accommodate the signature.
- Never cut the carrier sheet of a valuable print (unless the customer insists). The value of the piece is reduced or even cancelled by alteration of the original sheet.
- If artwork is mounted for stiffness within the frame, it **should** be spaced away from the glass with spacers or matting. If it is not, there is a strong tendency for it to stick to the glass and develop mold.

REPRODUCTIONS & POSTERS

- May be matted and/or dry mounted.
- Glass is not necessary if mounted, but must be used if matted.
- The white border on a print is a "carrier sheet" for handling purposes — it is not meant to show. When matting a reproduction, we usually do not show any white unless the customer insists.
- The "title block" is the nice printing centered on the bottom of the carrier sheet. It can be cut off and placed on the backside of the framed print, or there can be a hole cut in the mat for it to show through. Careful — do not cut it off without permission from the customer. If the information is left on the print under the mat, you may as well copy it onto a blank label and put it on the back of the framed piece — your customer will love you for it!
- The printed information on a show poster is often part of the poster and should be matted/framed to show it in its entirety. Of course trends change and so do a customer's feelings about the "words" on the poster. The words may be cut off or matted out to suit the customer.
- Some new posters have a very smooth glossy sheen — watch out — they have been printed on clay coated paper. The paper makes the printing ink colors look vibrant, however the smooth surface scratches easily, repels adhesives, and tends to make a smear-like mark on the glass, like the one left when you press your nose against a window.

WATERCOLORS/PEN & INK

- Both mediums are done on rather soft paper with water soluble media and both are subject to changes —moisture and humidity.
- The artwork may be buckled and wavy to begin with — had the artist treated the paper properly there would not be wavy watercolors and rippled pen and inks.
- The work must be matted to keep the surface from touching the glass. The mat usually rests on the edge of where the paint stops — the mat may overlap some of the paint edge due to the irregularity of the edge lines made by the painter. Pen and ink is generally centered on the page so the mat area is negotiable.
- To understand the reason for buckling on this type of work (also mixed media), picture the piece of paper the artist is using, then imagine the artist putting water in the center of the paper; the paper expands in the center when it gets wet so the ruffles around the edge are created by the center expansion. When you put the mat down on the work, the ruffled edge pushes in and creates buckles.

CHARCOALS & SOFT PASTELS & PENCIL DRAWINGS

- Delicate surface requires matting and glass.
- DO NOT USE ACRYLIC SHEETING. The static will transfer the artwork image onto the plastic.
- Careful of spray fixatives — they discolor and are not ever removable. Spray the surface ONLY if the customer insists. All sprays will eventually discolor.
- If the pastel work is heavy, a raised mat can be made by lifting the mat off the artwork with slices of foam centered board and attaching the artwork to the backboard. The extra chalk will fall into the gap. It will be difficult to handle — do not shake! Fit the work with an "expert fitting tool" so that the pastel will not be jarred.

OIL PASTELS

- Generally done on flimsy canvas type paper.
- Easiest and best handling is mat and glass; however, sometimes the customer thinks it is an oil painting. In that case it could be spray or wet mounted onto a board and framed without glass like an oil painting.

TEMPERA PAINTS

- Kids' stuff usually done on construction paper or newsprint. The paper will fade fast and become brittle. The paint remains water soluble, has little adhering qualities, cracks and falls off. Other than that, there's very little problem!

- Mat and glass picture if there are objects attached such as leaves and pieces of scrap materials. Take a moment and glue them down — library paste doesn't hold any better than it did when you were a kid!

RUBBINGS

- Usually done on thin craft paper (black) or Japanese paper (cream, white, tan).

- The image is made by rubbing a wax type crayon or paste on the face of the paper. The paper has been dampened and held on to the face of the brass or stone relief with tapes.

- This item cannot be dry mounted with heat — it will melt the wax media. You can iron the edges, wet mount, or wet or spray mount with a vacuum press.

- Keep image away from glass — use either mat or spacer.

PHOTOS

- Very delicate surface. Should be matted and glassed.

- The surface skin will stick to the glass if moisture gets into the frame job. Some have been treated with a spray which gives them a finish and helps to keep them from sticking to the glass. Glossy and slick finishes are more apt to stick to the glass than matte and linen finishes.

- Several products from a photo supply house will allow you to touch up scratches, etc. Stop in and ask for assistance.

- New RC paper from Kodak is resin coated to resist moisture changes. It does not mount as easily as the old papers; however, it can be dry mounted with heat or wet mounted (touchy).

- Larger pieces tend to "bowl" — when matted they will create a bulge in the center of the print. The same is true of home-developed photos, dry mounting will flatten them (if appropriate).

- Some photos have been mounted to a fabric/canvas and stretched over wooden stretcher bars and then brush stroked to simulate an oil painting. They can be put into a frame like an oil painting without glass. Caution: they are seldom square.

CERTIFICATES

- These should be handled relative to their worth. A Master's Degree, for example, should be treated like a valuable piece of artwork, with conservation in mind.

- Originally, certificates were printed on animal skins, also called parchment or vellum. While these words are also used to describe papers, the difference between the paper kind and the skin kind is readily visible. Because of their animal origin, skin certificates are difficult to handle. They expand and contract with environmental conditions. Conservation procedures would have you rag mat, hinge, and glass them. It is normal for skins to have wrinkles. If your customer insists on having them flattened, a skin can be wet mounted. Older skins brought to you for repair may have been wet mounted — it was once common practice. Dry mounting is possible but incredibly dangerous.

- Most paper certificates can be wet or dry mounted. Be careful of a new printing process that looks like engraving, but isn't. It is called thermograph printing and it melts under heat conditions, so do not heat mount.

- Should you need to replace a certificate (who, me?) most schools will sell you another one — just the paper ones, not the skin variety.

MIRRORS

- Can be purchased from most glass suppliers.

- 1/4" and 1/8" thicknesses are available. 1/8" is suitable for most frame jobs.

- Remember to paint the inside of the rabbet to match the frame (black is best) because the mirror reflects the inside of the rabbet.

- With a very heavy mirror you may want to use strong hangers on the back without wire. Provide the proper hooks for the wall and match up the heavy duty hangers on the backside of the frame. There will be better distribution of the weight and no chance of the wire breaking.

ERASERS

Great care should be taken when using erasers. There are many varieties available at art supply stores. Buy several. They will work differently depending on the type of papers and media. For example, art gum will work on most color printed surfaces, shiny or dull. A white vinyl eraser will erase almost any smudge. Careful — do not use it on color printed surfaces, it will erase the printing. A kneaded eraser is soft and pliable, it can be molded into any shape and used to "pick up" dirt. A rubber cement pick up is a 2" square that picks up rubbery glues and tape residue. The basic rules of using erasers: 1) secure the paper 2) use a clean eraser 3) test a corner 4) rub gently and slowly.

NEEDLEWORK & FABRIC

GENERAL INFORMATION ABOUT FABRIC ITEMS

- All fabrics must be stretched: needlepoint, cross-stitch, molas, batiks, crewel, embroidery, painting on fabrics, tapestries, scarves, etc.
- Mounting materials: if you use chipboard, put a layer of acid free board to cover. Use polyester batting for padding. It is inert and will not harm anything. Do not use foam-covered boards — they rot. Do not use "sticky-boards" — too permanent. Do not use plywood — too heavy and acidic.
- Whenever handling fabric pieces attach them in such a way that they can be un-attached without harm.
- For stretching purposes, 1-1/4" of extra fabric is needed to work with.
- Never cut a needlework — fold over extra material or ask the customer to cut it off before she leaves.
- When a piece is brought in — note the condition right away. Is it dirty, torn, finished?
- Needlepoints should not be glassed. It seals the natural fibers from necessary air circulation, causing mildew and rot.
- Glass is a matter of choice on thin fabric pieces. If you do use glass, some sort of spacer should be used to keep the piece from touching the glass.
- Antique pieces should be treated with the utmost care. Lightly sew them to an acid-free board or a natural linen material and then mount the linen.

- When an acid-free mounting board is needed you can use AFX or AF3X. These boards are double sided white acid-free mounting boards. The core as well as the surface papers are acid-free. They are available in several thicknesses. AFX is a single thick board while AF3X is double thick. 11W is a new needlework board that is white on both sides and has an acid-free core as well as face sheets, it is extra thick — 3/16 inch.
- Regular mounting boards are not acid-free but they may be useful in certain situations. 12C is an extremely thick, 3/16 inch, newsboard. It is very strong and dense. It will accept staples and pins. X is single thick while 3X is double thick. They both have a smooth finish with white acid-free surface paper on both sides.

  See pages 39 and 40 for additional boards.

NEEDLEWORK

MATTING A NEEDLEWORK

When using a mat on needlework, you will need to insert a spacer made of slices of mat board to compensate for the thickness of the fabric. The thicker the fabric to be matted the more spacing you will need. Attach the spacing with double faced tape at the outer edges of the unit. If you choose to pad the piece, cut the padding the size of the image of the needlework.

STRETCH MOUNTING A NEEDLEWORK

This is the most common method used by framers. It requires at least 1" of fabric all the way around the piece used in the stretching process. Padding will hide some of the irregularities of the stitchery but is not necessary. Note: some embroideries and crewel work will have long stitches on the backside where the needleworker carried the thread instead of tying it off. These long stitches will show through. You can have the customer clip and tie the threads or stretch it over a dark back ground to hide the color variations.

There are boards available that are thick enough to accept 1/4" staples or you could use several pieces of scrap mat board.

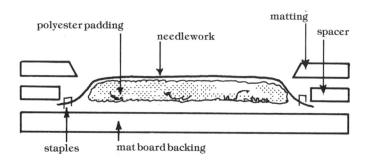

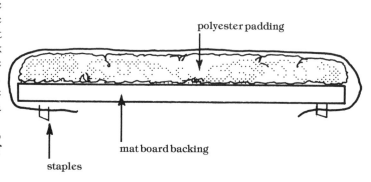

STRETCHING CANVAS & FABRIC

Materials required:
Hand gun stapler, staples, canvas pliers
or hammer and tacks.

1) Select stretcher bars (or make) the size you need — two of each. Fitted together, these four slotted bars form a frame on which to stretch your canvas or material.

2) Square the stretcher frame by lining it up against a carpenter's square.

3) You need about 1½" of canvas on each side for stretching. For example, a canvas to be stretched on 16" x 20" stretchers needs to be about 19" x 23".

4) Measure for the middle of each side of the canvas and the stretcher bar and mark with a pencil. This is very important to the successful stretching process.

5) Match up pencil marks on the sides, fold material margin over one of the short sides of the frame and fasten in the center with a staple gun.

6) Reverse to opposite side and stretch until canvas is taut and staple in the center.

7) Turn the frame with one of the longer sides up, grip and pull until you see diagonal wrinkles from the first two staples to the point where you are stretching, then staple in the center.

8) Repeat on the fourth side, pulling material until another pair of diagonal wrinkles appear to form a diamond shaped set of four wrinkles.

9) Move pliers a couple inches to the left of center staple and staple again. Repeat in the same direction, every two inches stapling towards the corner of the frame. Now do the same from the center to the right but stop about 3" from the corner.

10) Do the same on the opposite long side leaving 3" at the right end unfastened. Repeat on the two short sides.

11) Finish the corners last, folding the material under itself and pulling it snug. Staple securely.

12) Insert corner keys, two in each corner of the frame (longside of key against the wall) and tape lightly in place. As the painting ages the keys can be knocked into the slots, however it will disfigure the canvas. Some framers don't put them in — they use the keys to pick up nail hole filler!

If you don't want to staple directly into the fabric, you can sew extra material fabric onto the edges of the fabric and staple into that.

Do not trim off excess canvas.

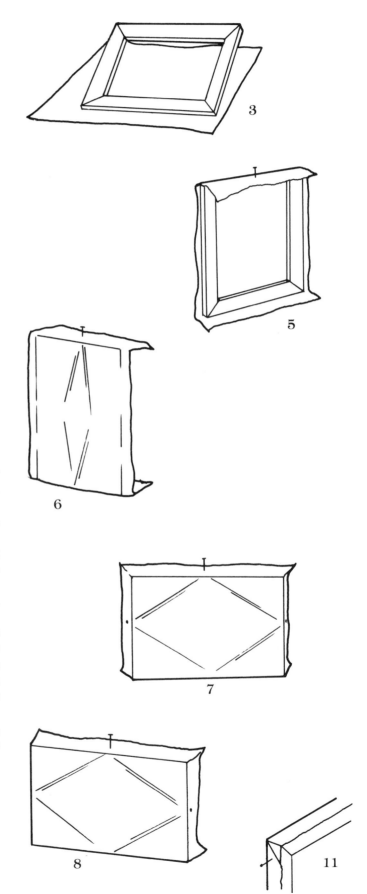

BLOCKING AND STRETCHING NEEDLEPOINT

Steam blocking will avoid any problems with bleeding yarns and cheap heavily sized canvas. It is also fast.

Materials:
- large wood panel marked off in 1″ blocks·
- staple gun
- steam iron

1) Line up side A and staple down (lightly).
2) Steam entire surface of needlepoint with a clean steam iron or steamer.
3) While the needlepoint is damp from the steam, pull side B to line up square and staple down to the board.
4) Steam entire needlepoint again and pull side C into alignment.
5) Line up side D and steam again.
6) Measure the needlepoint while it is on the board.
7) Cut boards for backing. You will need either one thick one or several 14 ply boards stacked together.
8) Cut polyester padding to same size as boards.
9) Remove the needlepoint from the wood blocking board and lay it face down and place the cut backing boards and polyester on the backside.
10) Fold flaps of canvas over edge of the padded board and staple at all four corners — pull firmly to keep it taut.
11) Check the front to keep the lines of the work even. Beginning in one corner, pull the work until you line up the canvas perfectly and then staple. Continue to staple around all the edges, positioning the staples very close together — the closer the smoother the stretch.

When you have a needlepoint that you do not want to use staples on, you can follow steps 1 to 9. Instead of using staples you can lace it. Lacing is similar to lacing your shoes. Using two pieces of yarn you zig zag from side to side and tighten as you go along.

In both cases, stapling or lacing, if you do not want to work directly on the canvas, you can sew an extra piece of material onto the canvas and do the stretching on the material.

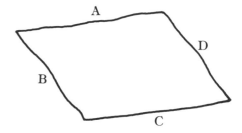

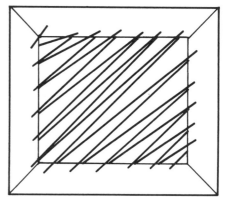

Lacing

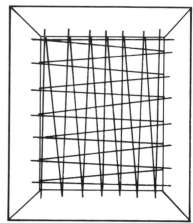

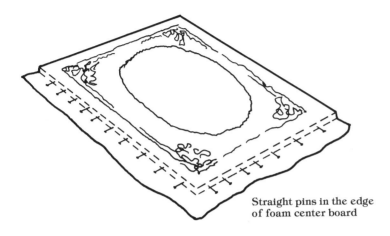

Straight pins in the edge
of foam center board

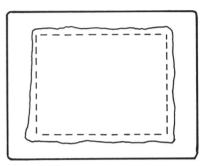

Stapled flat using an
office stapler

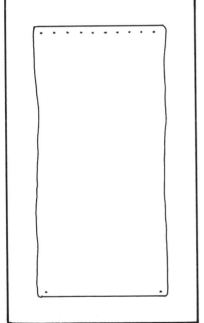

Sewn at the top.
Punch holes in the backing
board and sew through from
the backside

Loosely sew at the bottom to
keep it from moving. Careful
to allow room for material
to stretch out.

9
Inside the Frame Shop

Each shop owner must arrange showroom and workshop areas to suit individual needs. These needs are based on the type of framing produced, amount of space available, and types of goods retailed. For example, a shop that sells both art and picture framing will probably need more room than a shop that does just one or the other, and a gallery that sells antique prints will probably require less space than one that specializes in large contemporary paintings. The two would also require different types of back room space. If framing is not done on the premises, you will not need to devote a large area to framing — leaving more room for displaying and selling artwork.

The following is a list of areas, machines, and stock you may have in your shop. Many factors will determine your decisions. Machines may be chosen because of your knowledge of the products, or because of space limitations. Stock will be chosen based on services offered, and ability to buy, process, and store. Lounge, desk, and storage needs will depend on variables such as number of employees, amount of space available, and volume of work produced.

Here is a list of options to consider:

SHOWROOM
- desk, phone, file
- lounge area with chair, table, coffee, etc.
- cash register
- counter space
- mat board corner samples
- moulding display area
- container or area for pens, rulers, scratch paper, and work order blanks
- display areas for artwork and retail goods (print bins, display tables, etc.)

WORKROOM
- incoming goods "write-up" area
- storage for customers' goods (incoming)
- storage for customers' goods (finished)
- glass
- mat boards
- space for oversized boards and glass
- scrap board stock
- moulding
- chopper
- V-nailer
- joining table for vises
- vacuum press
- dry mount press
- spray booth
- lavatory
- furnace room
- water cooler, coffee machine area

- paper cutter
- trash containers
- work tables
- finished frame hangers
- nails and other hardware
- fabric storage — rolled and/or folded
- wall storage for stock moulding
- storage for incoming chops
- mat cutter
- oval cutter
- wall-mount board and glass cutter
- needlepoint blocking board
- storage for small tools
- storage cabinet for chemicals and sprays
- storage for tape, glue, paint, inks, and other small supplies
- storage for large paintings and frames
- fire extinguisher

Use graph paper and pencil-sketch your plan. Consider the traffic flow in your shop. For example, what jobs does your delivery door have to do? Will glass deliveries remain by the door? If the glass will be moved, how far do you have to move it?

A workroom is like a kitchen — it does not necessarily need more space to be most efficient. Bigger is not always better. Everything needs to be properly stored yet accessible. Spreading supplies around a large workroom may mean a lot of unnecessary travel time between operations. Organization is the key, especially when dealing with custom work. Handling your customer's belongings demands exacting care. You will need a consistent plan for tracking items through your shop so that they can be easily located at any time during the process.

FLOORING
Concrete floors are easy to clean, but they are very hard on the **feet** and **legs**. You will need rubber floor mats (from industrial supply companies) or pieces of carpeting placed where people will stand most often (or for long periods of time).

Wood floors are good for clean up, and easier on legs; but floor mats will still be helpful at the fitting table.

Carpeting is generally difficult to clean, but comfortable for standing — low nap would be the best choice.

Caution is advised in any area where glass shards may drop to the floor — they can stand upright when they fall onto carpeting or rubber mats, and can be very hazardous to your feet.

LIGHTING

Lots of light in the workroom, please. Fluorescent is the most economical, and casts an even, diffused light. There are several types of bulbs (tubes) to choose from. Use the sort that will give you the most natural, or daylight coloring. The "warm white" variety gives off the least ultraviolet rays (which are harmful to artwork). You may want to consider plastic sleeves made to cover the tubes, or a complete face sheet for the fixture, both of which filter out ultraviolet rays.

SAFETY PRECAUTIONS

Your shop should include the following:
- good ventilation
- fire extinguisher
- a cabinet for storage of chemicals and sprays
- goggles and masks
- first aid supplies
- saw guards
- proper electrical outlets for presses and compressors

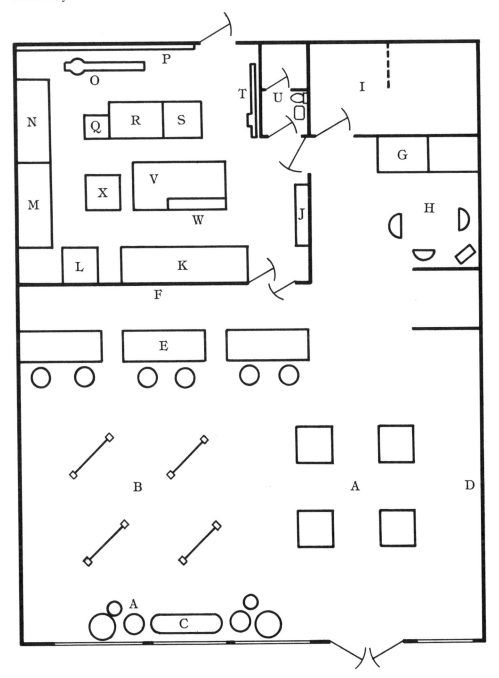

Gallery with frame shop
40' x 50'
2,000 sq. ft.
gallery 1,280 sq. ft.
frame shop 600 sq. ft.
offices 120 sq. ft.
Gallery:
a) display pedestals
b) island display for framed art
c) front window display
d) large display walls
e) design tables
f) corner samples
g) flat files
h) conversation area
i) offices
Workshop
j) large painting storage
k) finished goods storage
l) dry mt. press
m) incoming goods storage
n) mat board storage
o) chopper/saw
p) wall moulding rack
q) v-nailer
r) vise table
s) oval mat cutter
t) wall mtd. board cutter
u) lavatory & furnace room
v) work table
w) mat cutter
x) table paper cutter

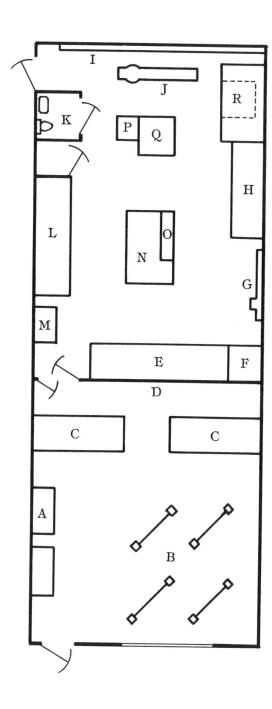

Frame Shop
20' x 50'
1,000 sq. ft.
Showroom 20' x 22'
440 sq. ft.
a) print bins
b) island display for
    framed art
c) design tables
d) corner samples
Workshop 20' x 28'
560 sq. ft.
e) finished goods
f) oval mat cutter
g) wall mtd. board cutter
h) mat board storage
i) wall moulding rack
j) chopper/saw
k) lavatory & furnace rm.
l) incoming goods
m) desk
n) work table
o) mat cutter
p) v-nailer
q) vise table
r) dry mt. press

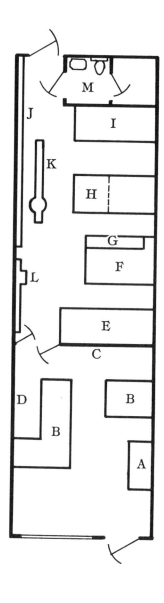

Frame Shop
12' x 40'
480 sq. ft.
Showroom 12' x 16'
192 sq. ft.
a) print bin
b) designing tables
c) corner samples
d) framing samples
Workshop
e) storage of customer's
    goods
f) work table
g) mat cutter
h) work table with
    dry mt. press
i) mat board storage
j) wall moulding rack
k) chopper/saw
l) wall mtd. board cutter
m) lavatory & furnace rm.

Each block = 1 ft.

Each block = 1 ft.

DESIGN YOUR OWN FLOOR PLANS

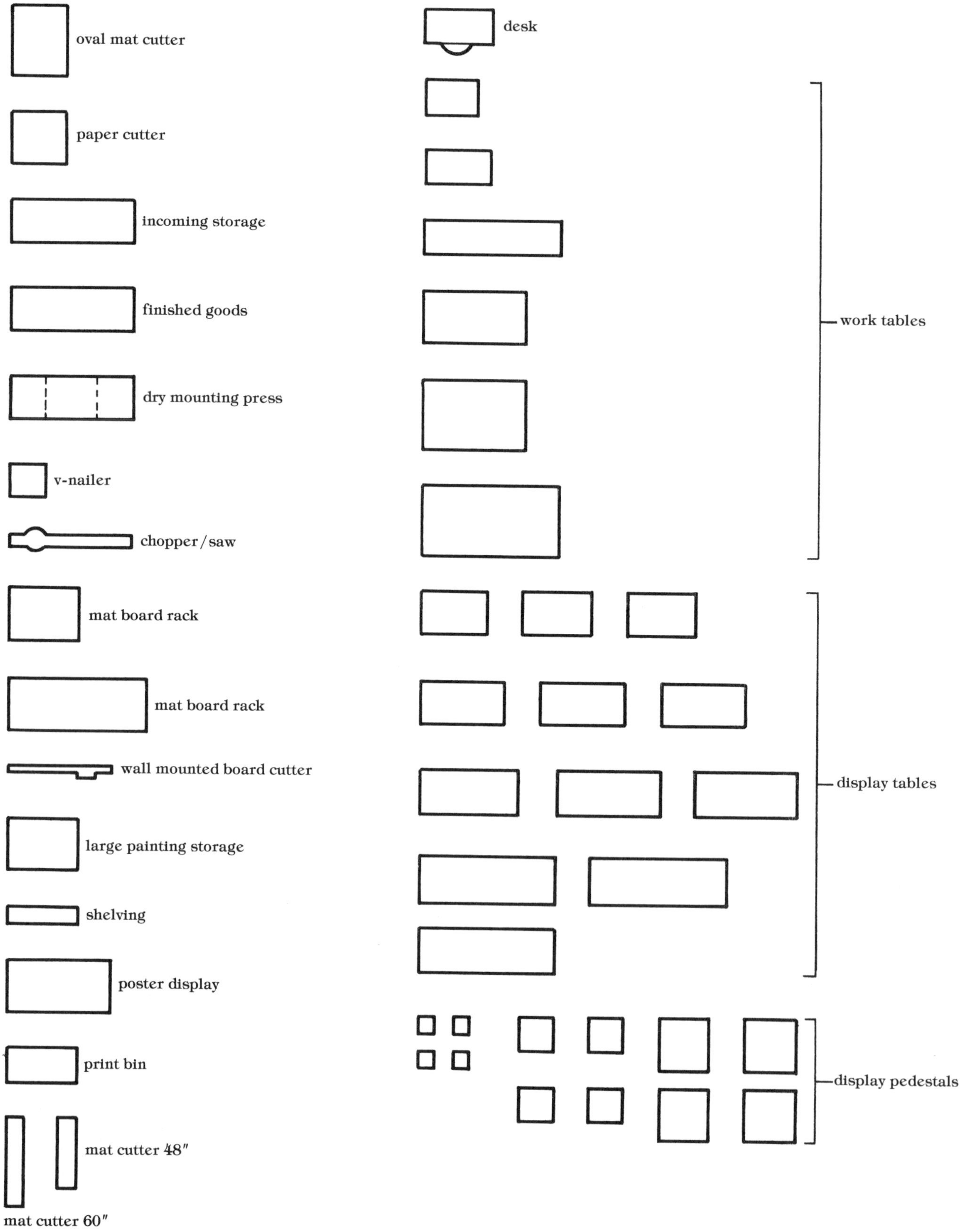

oval mat cutter

paper cutter

incoming storage

finished goods

dry mounting press

v-nailer

chopper / saw

mat board rack

mat board rack

wall mounted board cutter

large painting storage

shelving

poster display

print bin

mat cutter 48″

mat cutter 60″

desk

work tables

display tables

display pedestals

MOULDING STORAGE

VERTICAL STORAGE is possible if you have enough ceiling height to allow moulding lengths to stand up. Care should be taken to keep the moulding sticks upright and close to the wall, or unit, so that they will not warp. Vertical storage can be placed against the wall or shelving. A free-standing frame shelving unit can be made using wood or metal bracing. You can build one yourself or buy metal ones from industrial supply companies.

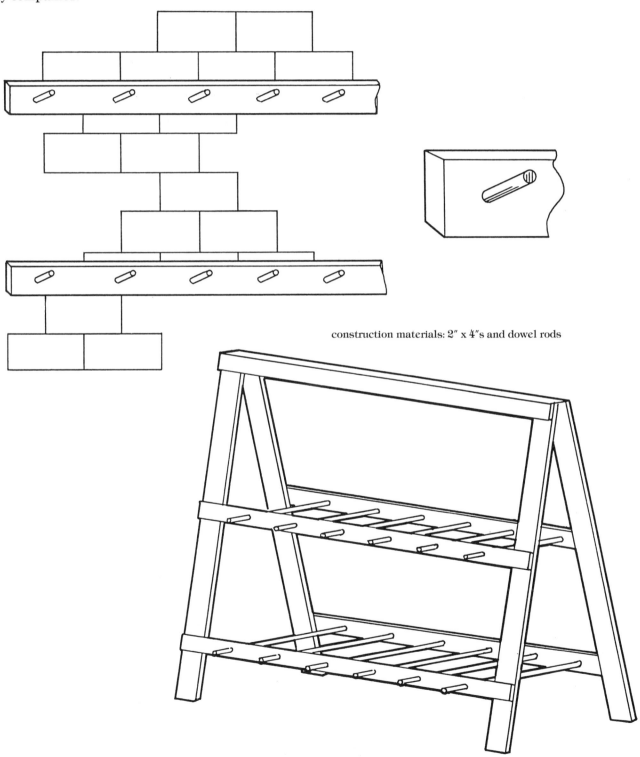

construction materials: 2″ x 4″s and dowel rods

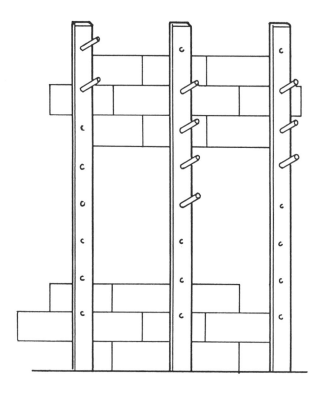

HORIZONTAL STORAGE can be placed against a wall, in pigeon holes or "H" frames. Horizontal storage will keep your moulding straight. However, it can make keeping track of "shorts" more difficult. If you are cramped for space, or if you have a basement operation, you can easily use the rafters to create horizontal storage space. Extend lath from the ceiling to make as many cubicles as the ceiling height will allow. If your ceiling is very high, you may require a ladder to reach the moulding.

attach to rafters

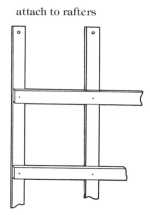

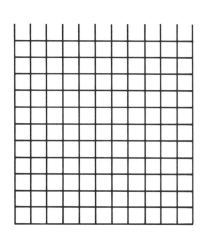

8' x 8' pigeon hole rack

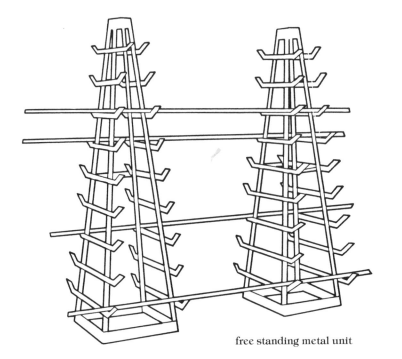

free standing metal unit

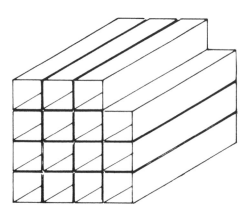

Cardboard boxes or tubes can be stacked to hold moulding. Tubes made of PVC piping could also be used.

STORAGE OF INCOMING customer goods is very important to an efficient, smooth running shop. Since your customers will bring in a wide variety of goods a storage system should be set up. This area is made of several ordinary units. Two flat files (cardboard or metal), several mailing tubes taped together, two file drawers, a large vertical shelving unit and a metal utility cabinet. Each area can be marked with a numeral or letter for easy identification.

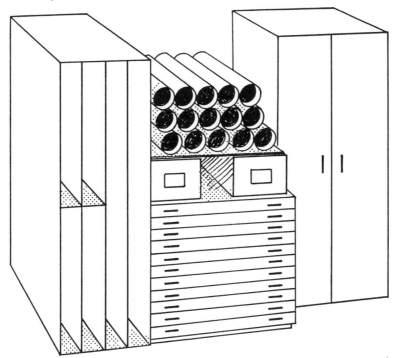

STORAGE OF FINISHED goods can be difficult because of the diversity of sizes, however this unit will take care of almost anything you've framed. The vertical shelving should have either carpet or scrap mat boards on each shelf so your completed frames do not scratch. Keep pieces of mat board or poster board between finished frames so they will not damage each other. The horizontal shelving will provide space for the smaller pieces. Again, a number or letter on each shelf will help locate a customer's finished order. Hint: Put numerals on one set and use the alphabet to mark the other. That way you'll know where to go right away.

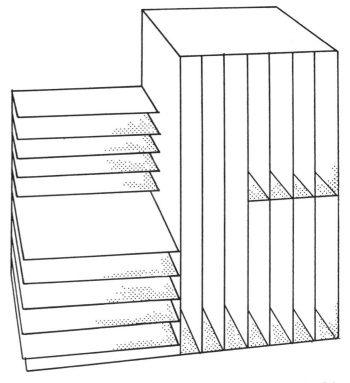

10

Work Orders

The function of the framing work order is to record and organize all the information pertaining to each framing job in a concise, regulated way. The efficiency of your work order form can make or break your work flow system. You must select or design a form tailored to the needs and style of your own shop.

There are many possible designs for a good work order. Some provide designated boxes for every piece of information that must be recorded (a grocery list), while others provide mostly blank lines, where information can be listed according to a shop's preferred system. A beginner will appreciate the box-checking method, and it can help to prevent confusion; but well-trained salespeople will have no problem with, and may prefer the freedom of, the more flexible, unstructured order form.

The size of the form may vary from rather small such as 4¼" x 7" to a full 8½" x 14". Check with your printer to make sure the size you choose is an economical size for printing. Although a framing order form requires that a lot of information fit neatly on one piece of paper there are any number of ways to accomplish this task successfully, even on the smaller sized forms.

The number of copies you need depends on how you decide to handle the work processing system. At least two copies are recommended as the minimum. However, three should work out perfectly. You may use carbons, or NCR (carbonless) paper, which is less messy. Forms are available with color coded copies which are a convenient way to put the proper form in its proper place.

Regardless of data on your work orders, there are a number of basic essentials you must include, and several optional elements to consider.

BUSINESS ESSENTIALS

Shop Name, Address, and Phone Number

Be sure to include all three. Your customers should not have to search for this information. You may have the information printed on the form, or stamp it on with a rubber stamp; the latter is less expensive but less professional looking.

Customer's Name and Phone Number

Get the address too, if desired. If your shop is open mostly during daytime hours, you may need your customer's work phone number as well as home phone. Ask for a daytime number or a number where he or she can most often be reached. This is more polite than asking specifically for a home number or work number and it avoids discussion about the customer's employment status.

Date Received

Always know when the work came to you.

Date Due

Or whatever pickup method you decide to use. This should be made very clear both on the order form and verbally to the customer. Provide either a space marked "Due Date" or a printed statement such as "will phone when completed." Phoning all your customers can become very time consuming — time that could be used selling or framing.

Prices and Totals

Some forms provide only one space for the total amount of the order; but in the interest of clarity and accuracy, it is probably better to show the breakdown of pricing directly on the order form — including space for the cost of each element of the framing job, with room provided for tax, totals, and deposits to be credited.

FRAMING ESSENTIALS

However you decide to arrange these elements, remember to make the frame information prominent, then follow some logical sequence with the other categories.

Frame

Record the source and size, using whatever system you have chosen to specify moulding. Remember to provide a space for liner frames, too.

Mounting

Show the type of mounting desired (wet, dry, etc.) and perhaps the type of mounting surface, such as foam-center board or white mounting board.

Matting

Record color and board type. Remember to allow space for recording this information for multiple mats.

Glass

Record type desired — regular, nonglare, Plexiglas, etc.

Labor Charges

This refers to fitting, which includes the cost of filler boards, hangers, and other materials used in the fit job. You may also want to provide a space for recording the type of hanger preferred by the customer, such as sawtooth or screw eyes and wire.

Measurements

Some shops draw sketches or show mathematics. Some forms have pre-printed pictures with blank spaces for recording dimensions. Others simply state the outside measurement and the desired mat border. There are many good ways to organize this portion of the order form, but keep this in mind: there are many variables involved in this category, so you must establish a well-defined method for recording all mat borders, shapes of mat openings, number of mat openings, placement of openings, and outside dimensions. The salesperson or designer should specify exact measurements and be responsible for them. If the framers have to remeasure everything it will waste time.

Special Services

This includes services such as shadow boxes, blocking, stretching, repairs, cleaning, etc. If these are services you provide regularly, you may want to give them designated placements on your order form.

Type of Artwork

Always record this somewhere on the form. Even if you prefer the checklist style of form, a blank space marked "description" or "item" handles this most efficiently, to allow for the wide variety of pieces your shop may encounter.

Special Instructions

Providing a space for this is very important and recommended for every work order form. There are many cases when customers will make unusual requests, such as "do not flatten creases in print," or when salespeople want to let the framer know about some special feature of the job.

All work orders should be filled out properly so that any framer or salesperson can figure out the intent — do not allow people to write "see me" on the form because they think it's too complicated to write — there is nothing more frustrating than to start to work on a job and not have the full information. No excuses — write it down!

OPTIONS

Claim Check

It is important to give every customer some sort of receipt at the time the order is placed. If your work order form does not provide a copy of the entire order for the customer, then provide a claim slip at the bottom of your form — this can be perforated to tear off easily. A customer's receipt should contain the following information: order number, due date, customer's name, price totals, shop name and phone number. The advantage of giving the customer a copy of the entire order is that there will be no confusion later about prices and framing choices. On the other hand, you as the framer may have to make some "adjustments" to the work order (tampico brown vs. malay mat color); also the customers are sometimes put-off by the breakdown of prices (drymounting is how much?) whereas the total for the whole job may sound reasonable to them.

Order Number

Your work order should be numbered. Numbering helps keep multiple orders from the same customer separate and distinguishable from one another besides giving the whole system order and accountability.

Salesperson

Initials will do. This is important in a shop where more than one person will be taking in the frame orders.

Payment Method

Cash, credit card, to be billed, etc.

Condition

Describe defects present in artwork when customer presents the piece to you. Salespeople should always scan artwork for problems like scratches, stains, or tears, and mention them (politely) to the customer, then record them on the work order.

Disclaimer

This may release you from responsibility in certain situations. For example, you may wish to have a statement that says "accepted and agreed to" or "not responsible for goods after 90 days" or "customer decided against conservation measures." You have to be careful of disclaimers — they may scare your customers and they may also not be valid because of state laws requiring a certain level of service and responsibility.

CŒK'S Art Supplies & Custom Framing

4366 PORTAGE AVE. **PHONE 216/494-7730** **NORTH CANTON, OHIO 44720**

• PORTFOLIOS • PADS AND MAT BOARD **Nº 1837**

PHONE	CREDIT CARD NO		DATE RECEIVED	DATE PROMISED

NAME

ADDRESS				ZIP CODE

DESCRIPTION OF ITEM TO BE FRAMED			DECLARED VALUE $	

ITEM	DESCRIPTION			AMOUNT
FRAME	SIZE	MOLDING NO	NO. OF FEET / PRICE FOOT	$
LINER	SIZE	NO	NO. OF FEET / PRICE/FOOT	
MAT #1	NO./TYPE	COLOR	MARGINS T S B	
MAT #2	NO./TYPE	COLOR	MARGINS T S B	
MAT #3	NO./TYPE	COLOR	MARGINS T S B	
GLASS	☐ REGULAR ☐ PLEXI ☐ MIRROR ☐ NON-GLARE ☐ ACRYLIC ☐			
MOUNT	☐ DRY ☐ MUSEUM TYPE OF BACKER ☐ WET ☐			
HANGER	☐ WIRE ☐ EASEL ☐ SAWTOOTH ☐			
MISC. SERVICES	☐ STRETCH ☐ REPAIR ☐ ☐ BLOCK ☐ FITTING			
MISC. SUPPLIES				

SPECIAL INSTRUCTIONS	SUB-TOTAL	
	TAX	
	TOTAL	
	DEPOSIT	
	BALANCE DUE	

I hereby authorize the above work to be done, with any materials or supplies required. Recognizing that extreme care will be taken with the article(s) being framed, I agree to assume all risks and liabilities. I understand the shop is not responsible for work left over 30 days.

CUSTOMER'S SIGNATURE _____ DATE _____

This work order is a "grocery list" type form with one blank area for special instructions. Note the "disclaimer," requiring the customer's signature, at the bottom. The form has three copies.

The first goes to the customer, the second into a file and the third goes with the art work. The third copy is made of card stock and has the drawings of mats on the backside. The top two copies are made of regular paper.

FRAME & MAT DIMENSIONS

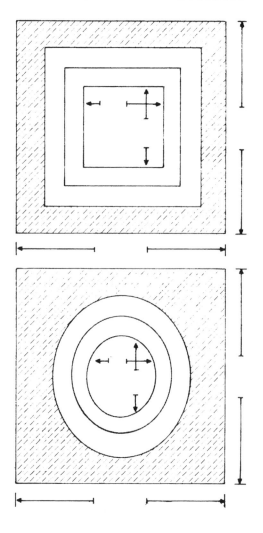

82518

NAME			SP
PHONE		DATE / /	

QTY.	FRAME		PRICE/FOOT	AMOUNT
	LINER			
CHP	SIZE			

	SEE SPECIAL INSTRUCTIONS ATTACHED	
	CUSTOMER ELECTED NOT TO USE MUSEUM PROCEDURES	
	DEPOSIT	

ITEM	VALUE

ACCEPTED AND AGREED TO

- -

Kistler Art   _____

DATE PROMISED
CLAIM CHECK

This work order is from a shop that does custom framing. There are three copies, one goes with the frame (chop, cut in house, or ready-made), the second goes with the art, the third goes into a Master File in order to control all orders in the shop. The salesperson is expected to accurately measure and record all information on the form and use the blank area to illustrate or explain special jobs. The customer's receipt is a 1″ tear-off at the bottom of the first copy. The salesperson will write the price plus tax along with the number of the order and the due date before tearing it off.

20- 21899

		DIY	CUSTOM	CALL	EST	TO ORDER
NAME		H P			C L K	
ADDRESS		W P			B I N	

S U B				
M O U L D				
P R I C E				
U I		# F T		
T A B L E				

		PAGE	OF	

	MAT	UPPER	LOWER	LOWEST
COLOR				
TOP				
SIDES				
BOTTOM				
G L A S S	REG	N G	S I Z E	

SPECIAL INSTRUCTIONS

	LINER
	MOULDING
	MAT
	MAT
	MAT
	OVAL MULTI
	GLASS
	HARDWARE
	BACKING BOARD
	MOUNTING BOARD
	DRY MOUNT
	CONSERVATION
	EASEL
	OTHER
X	SUB TOTAL
	TOTAL

MATERIALS _____

LABOR/SHOP FEE _____

RETAIL _____

SUB TOTAL _____

TAX _____

TOTAL _____

DEPOSIT _____

BALANCE DUE _____

The Framer's Workshop
DO IT YOURSELF CUSTOM FRAMING

• 1658 BRITTAIN ROAD   AKRON, OH 44310
(216) 630-2512

• 25 GHENT ROAD   AKRON, OH 44313
(216) 867-1662

• 4925 WHIPPLE AVE. NW   CANTON, OH 44718
(216) 492-9922

DATE	DATE DUE

ORIGINAL

This work order is from a shop that offers both DIY (do-it-yourself) and custom framing. It is a three part form. The original follows the work, the second copy goes to accounting, and the third goes to the customer. This is a "grocery list" type of form. It lists all the services that your shop performs. Your salesperson checks off the types of services this particular job requires. There are two blank areas for explanation and illustration.

ARTCOMP, Inc.
CUSTOM FRAMING WORK ORDER

DUE :04/25/85
=================

CUSTOMER :REDLICH
ART..KELLY

ORDER DATE: 04/14/85

SPECIFICATIONS

FRAME	7V10300 @ Bin- 10	
	11 Feet Required	
OUTSIDE MAT	WTE	
INSIDE MAT	4785 1/8 LIP	
GLASS	REGULAR GLASS	
MOUNT	MOUNT ON X-BOARD	
OTHER REQMTS	FRAMESPACE	
IMAGE SIZE	24 x 28 3/4	

This work order is a computer generated form. You type into the machine what you want done on the job and it will be printed on two forms. One will be a work sheet, the other a price sheet which shows the total price of the frame job and a separate price for the purchased art. This form was printed with one copy of each sheet.

=============================
=============================

28 1/2 x 32 3/4
=============================

MAT WIDTH--TOP 2

=============================

MAT WIDTH--BOTTOM 2 1/2--SIDE 2

175

ARTCOMP, Inc.   138
P.O. BOX 787
Woodland Hills, CA 91367
818-888-1963

CUSTOMER: MR & MRS N **REDLICH**
ADDRESS: 6047 ROD AVE
WOODLAND HILLS, CA 91367
ORDER DATE: 04/14/85

PHONE No.-:

DUE: **04/25/85**

ORDER	DESCRIPTION	PRICE

175	Frame-KELLY	$ 162.73

	SUB-TOTAL	$ 162.73
	LESS DISCOUNT @ 10 %	16.27
	POSTER	75.00

	TOTAL	$ 221.46
Not Responsible if	SALES TAX	14.39
Left Over 90 Days		-------
	GRAND TOTAL	$ 235.85
	PAYMENT (M/C)	200.00

THANK YOU	**BALANCE**	$ 35.85

FRAME by globex

SHOP ORDER

Customer Name : PAT BRADY

Telephone No. :

Order No.   : 1037 1/1

Date of Order : 05/23/85

Date Promised : 06/10/85

Description : DOG PRINT   Horizontal

```
        No. Required    :  1

        Picture Size    : 14.500  x 16.250

        MARGINS  Top    : 3.000
                 Left   : 3.000
                 Right  : 3.000
                 Bottom : 3.000

        Opening Size    : 20.500  X  22.250

        Frame Number    : HO-257
             Width      : 1.50

        Top Mat Type    : 1
             No.        : 912
             Color      : INDIA

        Middle Mat Type :
             No.        :
             Color      :

        Bottom Mat Type : 1
             No.        : 1056
             Color      : BLD BRN

        Bottom Mat Lip  : .25
        Top Mat Lip     : .

        Glass Type      : Clear

        LABOR  X Building        X Fitting        Refitting

               Stretching          Blocking

               X Drymounting     X FOMCOR        SPECIAL
```

This work order is turned out by a computer. You can have the form customized to suit your needs when you buy the software. This one gives all the pertinent information along with a check off area at the bottom of the order form. Your computer can either print you multiples or you could have a terminal at the framer's desk where she can look up the file. Note: there are no prices on this page. With this type of program the prices could be added on.

FRAME Ordered/Cut ____   Made ____   MAT(s) ____   GLASS Ordered/Cut ____   COMPLETE ____

FRAME by globex

PROCESSING FRAMING ORDERS

How to take in work, know where it is, what is needed to complete it, when to work on it, when it must be finished, and where to put it when it is finished.

To create an efficient, professional atmosphere in your shop, you must be able to quickly answer all of the above questions. Even a small business benefits from an organized work flow system. Let's follow a piece of artwork through the entire process.

The process begins with the customer, who brings in a piece of artwork and orders a frame job. When the various framing decisions are confirmed, you write up the work order, clearly specifying every aspect of the job. The customer is given some sort of receipt — a claim check or copy of the work order.

Next, protect the artwork: wrap it, or place it in a folder, bag, box — whatever is necessary to store it safely. Attach a copy of the work order to the package (**not** to the face of the artwork — it could make marks on the artwork). This copy stays with the piece through the entire process.

Record the order in a Schedule Book on the date it is **due**. The schedule book is essential to the system and should include: the customer's name; the nature of the artwork; the size and identity of the frame; space for

indicating where the artwork was stored before framing, and where it was placed when finished. (Note — it is helpful to use numbering for incoming storage spaces and lettering for outgoing, or vice-versa.) Add anything else you think is important to your schedule book design. It is useful to indicate whether mounting will be done, and it may be convenient to include a small space where back orders can be noted. The schedule book should **always** remain in its designated area, preferably on a shelf or table with space nearby, where artwork (with work orders attached) can be safely placed during busy parts of the day, until you have time to complete the scheduling. Place the artwork in the appropriate storage space.

*Note — Alternatives to the schedule book include clipboard listing systems, however, these can become obsolete in a hurry when business increases. Other shops have used a wall-mounted calendar for scheduling work, similar to the method used in many car repair shops. This can be sloppy, and can cause space problems when the work schedule gets heavy (overfilling the space provided on the calendar). If work sheets are attached to the calendar, a fallen or lost slip means there is no record of the work scheduled!

Now, order your frame. You need to allow for all of the possibilities your shop offers — ready-made frames, custom frames from stock moulding, chop frames. If your work order system provides a sheet for the frame, attach this sheet to ready-made frames, and hang them in a specified area. Provide boxes marked accordingly to hold the order sheets for frames that must be custom-made or ordered. If you do not have a work order copy for the frame, you will need an organized listing sheet on which all frames are recorded, and a labeling system to indicate which frame belongs to which customer — this is essential when dealing with many orders simultaneously.

If your work order provides a sheet for filing, place it in an alphabetized master file of work in progress. This comes in handy when customers phone to check on orders, when employees must phone customers, or when customers forget claim slips. At this point, the initial processing is completed.

Some days later, the framer checks the schedule book and sees that your customer's order is due. The artwork is stored in section 4. The framer locates the piece and its attached worksheet. The frame happens to be a metal-section frame, so the framer goes to the area of the workroom designated for metal frames, and locates the one with your customer's name on it. The framer follows the instructions indicated on the work order, and completes the job. The finished piece is placed in storage, and its location is marked in the schedule book.

Now, the customer calls to make sure her work is ready. If you have a master file, you can find the cus-tomer's order sheet, and use it to check the status of the job in the schedule book. If the customer has her claim slip (showing due date) handy, you can forego the file box and head right for the schedule book. If there is no master file and the customer has lost her claim slip (which seems to happen rather often), you will just have to search the schedule book until you find the right name! It takes time, especially if there are lots of names, and is not the preferred method.

Let's say this customer has her claim check. You find her name in the schedule book and see that the work is completed, and report the good news to the customer. She comes to the shop the next day, and another salesperson waits on her. The finished work is easily located, following the same procedure used to determine the work's readiness when the customer called the day before. The salesperson goes to the storage space indicated, finds the piece, and brings it to the customer, who is quite pleased with the beauty and quality of your work.

Remember, a framing business requires that customers **trust you** with their artwork. A comfortable, casual, atmosphere in your shop makes customers feel welcome; but don't mistake inefficient for easy-going. Beware of confusion and sloppiness in your work flow system that can endanger the shop's credibility.

Different styles work in different shops. Design a processing system that suits your individual needs and preferences. If you can quickly determine the status and location of the piece and its frame at any point in the process, then your system works!

Your schedule book can look like this:

SOURCES

The following companies have contributed not only to this book but to the picture framing industry. We appreciate their innovation, research and products.

Accent Art Distributors Ltd.
#302
294 East 1st Ave.
Vancouver, British Columbia
Canada V5T 1A6

Andrews/Nelson/Whitehead
31-10 48th Ave.
Long Island City, NY 11101

Art Business News
60 Ridgeway Plaza
Stamford, CT 06905

ArtComp, Inc.
6047 Rod Ave.
Woodland Hills, CA 91367

Artique Mat Cutter
1115 Bunker Hill Rd.
Cookeville, TN 38501

Artisan Frame & Moulding Co.
4695 Winchester Rd.
Memphis, TN 38116

Artistic Larson-Juhl
5830 Coopers Ave.
Mississauga, Ontario
Canada L4Z 1Y3

Art-O-Rama, Inc.
510 Fifth Ave.
Pelham, NY 10803

Carithers International Assoc.
5752-A Gallant, POB 16997
Jackson, MS 39206

Cook's Art Supply & Custom Framing
4366 Portage Rd. N.W.
N. Canton, OH 44720

Crescent Cardboard Co.
100 W. Willow Rd.
Wheeling, IL 60090

DECOR Magazine
408 Olive St.
St. Louis, MO 63102

Denton Vacuum, Inc.
(Denglas)
2 Pin Oak Ave.
Cherry Hill, NJ 08003

Designer Moulding
6910 Preston Hwy.
Louisville, KY 40219

The Fletcher-Terry Co.
65 Spring Ln.
Farmington, CT 06032

Flex-Form, Inc.
1480 Landmeier Rd.
Elk Grove Village, IL 60007

Industrial Saw
2 Merle Ave.
Oceanside, NY 11572

Ivy Industries, Inc.
P.O. Box 7747
Charlottesville, VA 22906

Larson-Juhl
4320 International Blvd.
Norcross, GA 30093

Lineco Inc.
P.O. Box 2604
Holyoke, MA 01041

Abe Munn/Frame Guild
51-02 21st St.
Long Island City, NY 11101

Northcoast Frame Supply
2479 Russell St.
Cuyahoga Falls, OH 44221

Piedmont Moulding
P.O. Box 117
Conyer, GA 30207

Pistorius Machine Co.
1785 Express Dr. N.
Hauppauge, NY 11788

Alfred Schiftan, Inc.
406 W. 31st St.
New York, NY 10001

Seal Products
550 Spring St.
Naugatuck, CT 06770

3M Company
3M Center, COSD
Bldg. #223-3S
St. Paul, MN 55144

ViraTec
(TruVue Glass)
1315 N. North Branch St.
Chicago, IL 60622

TRADE ASSOCIATIONS:

Professional Picture Framers Assoc.
4305 Sarellen Rd.
Richmond, VA 23231

Australian Picture Framers Assoc
19 Glenferrie Ave.
Cremorne 2090
Australia

National Art Materials Trade Assoc.
178 Lakeview Ave.
Clifton, NJ 07011

American Institute for Conservation
The Klingle Mansion
3545 Williamsburg Lane N.W.
Washington, D.C. 20008

The Fine Art Trade Guild
16-18 Empress Place
London SW6 1TT
England

The Institute of British Picture Framers
5 Elm Close
Amersham, Buckinghamshire
England   HP6 5DD

BIBLIOGRAPHY

"Basic Information Series, Number 4: Wood." Profitable Craft Merchandising, September, 1976 p. 43.

Clapp, Anne E. Curatorial Care of Works of Art on Paper. Third Edition. Intermuseum Conservation Association, 1978.

Dawes, Wallace. The Collector as Curator in Today's World. The Paper Mill, Division of Shiva, Inc., 1983.

DECOR Magazine. The Freshman Framer, Books 1, 2, and 3. Commerce Publishing, 1981.

DECOR Magazine. Modern Matting: The Framer's Guide to Decorative Matting Techniques. Commerce Publishing, 1983.

Frederick, Paul. The Framer's Answer Book. Commerce Publishing for DECOR Magazine, 1980.

Frederick, Paul. More Answers For the Framer. Commerce Publishing for DECOR Magazine, 1981.

Grimm, Claus. The Book of Picture Frames. Abaris Books, 1981.

Heydenryk, Henry. The Art and History of Frames. James H. Heineman, Inc., 1963.

Hunter, Dard. Papermaking: The History and Technique of an Ancient Craft. Dover Publications, 1978.

Maffeo, Thomas. How to Dry Mount, Texturize, and Protect with Seal. Seal 1981.

Mayer, Ralph. The Artist's Handbook of Materials and Techniques. 3rd ed. New York: The Viking Press 1974.

National Art Materials Trade Association. Paper and Boards, Training Manual No. 4. NAMTA, 1979.

"Paper Facts: Understanding Art Papers." The Paper Mill, Division of Shiva, Inc.

Plenderleith, H. J., and Werner, A. E. A. The Conservation of Antiquities and Works of Art. Second Edition. Oxford University Press, 1979.

Professional Picture Framer's Association. PPFA Guild Guidelines for Framing Works of Art on Paper. PPFA, 1985.

M. Smith, N. Jones, II, S. Page and M. Dirda. "Pressure Sensitive Tape and Techniques for its Removal from Paper." Journal of the American Institute for Conservation Vol. 23 (Spring 1984): 101 to 113.

Wright-Smith, Rosamund. Picture Framing. Van Nostrand Reinhold, 1980.

Zigrosser, Carl, and Gaehde, Christa M. A Guide to the Collecting and Care of Original Prints. Crown Publishers for the Print Council of America, 1975.

Index